POSITION OF THE DAY PLAYBOOK

REVISED AND UPDATED

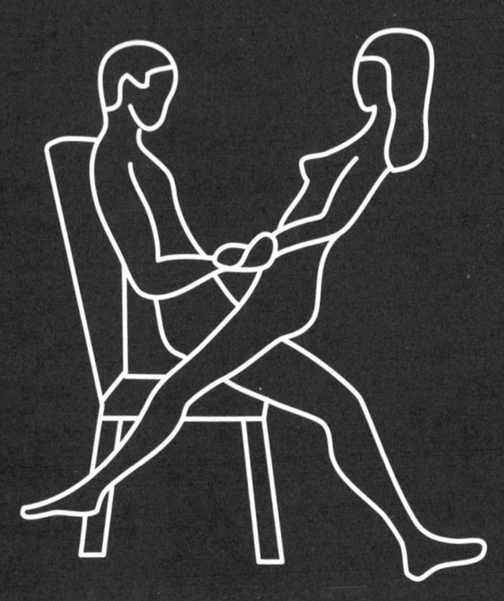

POSITION OF THE DAY
PLAYBOOK
SEX EVERY DAY IN EVERY WAY

CHRONICLE BOOKS
SAN FRANCISCO

Library of Congress Cataloging-in-Publication Data available.

ISBN 978-1-7972-3723-7

Manufactured in India.

Design by Erik Olsen Graphic Design.
Typesetting by Wynne Au-Yeung.

10 9 8 7 6 5 4 3 2 1

Chronicle Books LLC
680 Second Street
San Francisco, California 94107
www.chroniclebooks.com

INTRODUCTION

Welcome to *Position of the Day: Playbook*, *Nerve.com*'s guide to a life of sexual inventiveness. When we published the first *Position of the Day*, we received a lot of feedback. Most of the people who bought the book were thrilled to have so many new ways to spice up their sex lives. Others said they loved the titles of the positions but couldn't always manage to, *umm*, make them work right. A few people got stuck in the positions and were in need of emergency assistance.

We were especially surprised by how many questions people had about the positions: What are the pros and cons of doing "The Knee-Jerk Reaction" (June 25) or "The Munchies" (July 7)? Do any of the positions work better with props or equipment—say a bench or a swing? And, hey, do I still need to go to the gym if I'm regularly having sex upside down with my head on a chair and my feet wrapped around my lover's neck?

We've tried to address as many of these concerns as possible by adding a handy rating system so you can keep track of which positions work best for you. Listing the equipment you might need and the various hazards and benefits of the different positions was easy. But questions about what sort of workout you get from having sex "every day in every way" kept us up at night worrying. So we decided to figure out how long the average sex act lasts and which muscles are used in a given position. We planned to send a team of nimble volunteers down to the laboratory and strap all sorts of wires to their bodies to observe them having sex in hundreds of different positions. But then we remembered that we weren't scientists and just came up with our best estimates for the numbers of calories you'll burn.

We hope you'll have as much fun with this book as we had putting it together. This newly revised edition includes all the classics, plus reimagined positions and essential updates—ensuring that sex can be fun and inclusive for everyone! And remember, if you happen to get stuck in any of the positions, a little melted butter can go a long way.

—The *Nerve* Staff

NERVE.COM

Nerve was a popular online magazine about sex, relationships, and culture. Founded in 1997, *Nerve* published award-winning essays, provocative photography, and stimulating reporting for nearly two decades. Described by *Entertainment Weekly* as "*Playboy*'s body with *The New Yorker*'s brain," the website won numerous awards, including National Magazine Award nominations and Webby Awards.

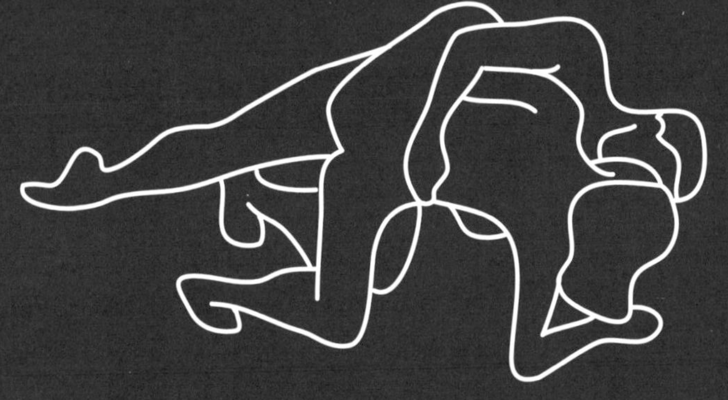

THE POSITIONS

JANUARY 01)
THE STROKE OF MIDNIGHT

CALORIES
Giver 19
Receiver 13.6

EQUIPMENT
Champagne
Glasses
Confetti

BENEFIT
Fresh Start

- ○ Below Average
- ○ Average
- ○ Above Average
- ○ Whoa!

COMMENTS

JANUARY 02)

LOVE IS BLIND

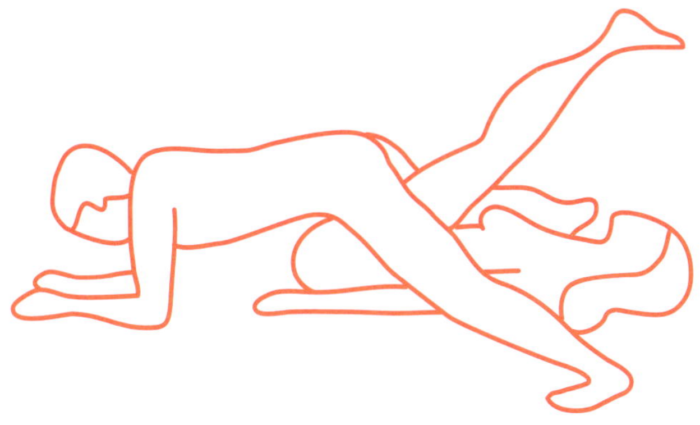

CALORIES
Giver 75.6
Receiver 96

EQUIPMENT
Optional:
Newspaper

BENEFIT
Hamstring
Workout

- ○ Below Average
- ○ Average
- ○ Above Average
- ○ Whoa!

COMMENTS

JANUARY 03)
THE CHIMNEY SWEEP

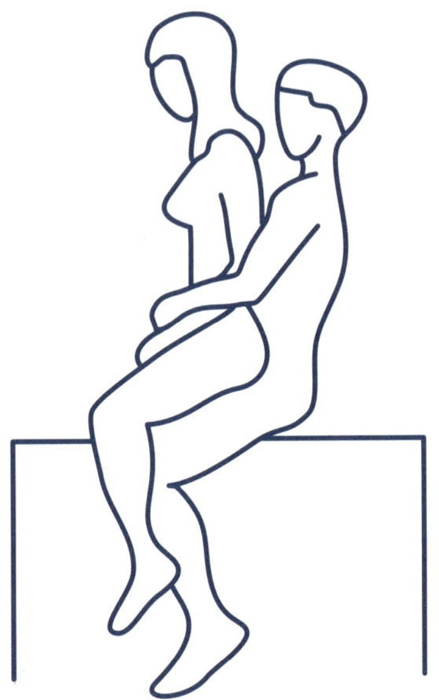

CALORIES
Giver 67.2
Receiver 48

EQUIPMENT
Chimney

HAZARD
Soot

○ Below Average
○ Average
○ Above Average
○ Whoa!

COMMENTS

JANUARY 04)
YOU PLUS ME

CALORIES

Giver 100.8
Receiver 96

- ○ Below Average
- ○ Average
- ○ Above Average
- ○ Whoa!

COMMENTS

JANUARY 05)

THE AMUSE-BOUCHE

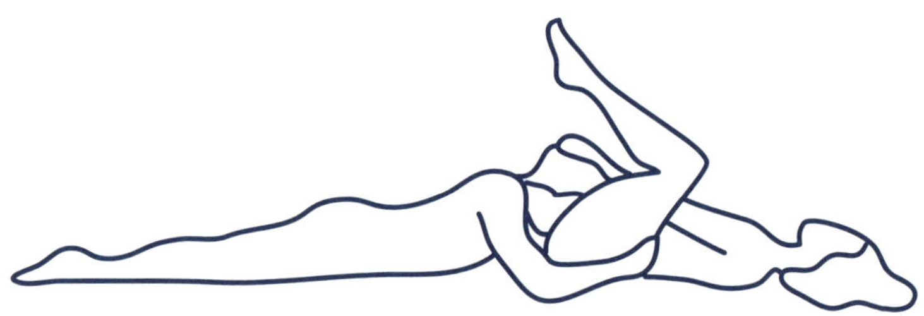

CALORIES		BENEFIT
Giver	19	Low Carb
Receiver	48	

- ○ Below Average
- ○ Average
- ○ Above Average
- ○ Whoa!

COMMENTS

JANUARY 06)

THE TROPHY SHELF

CALORIES

Giver 19

Receiver 54

- ○ Below Average
- ○ Average
- ○ Above Average
- ○ Whoa!

COMMENTS

JANUARY 07)

THE TICKLER

CALORIES		HAZARD
Giver	75.6	Giggling Fits
Receiver	54	

- ○ Below Average
- ○ Average
- ○ Above Average
- ○ Whoa!

COMMENTS

JANUARY 08)

PUPPY LOVE

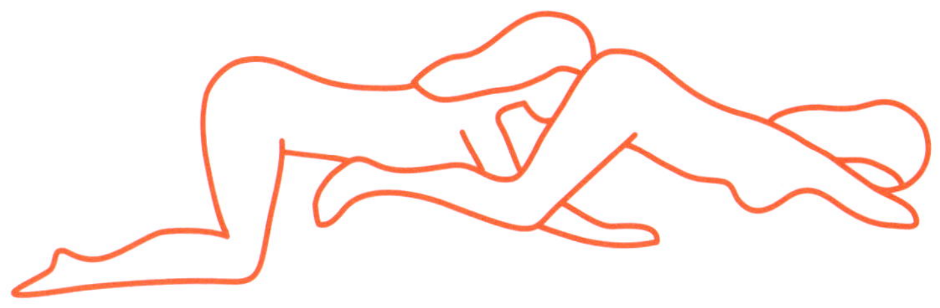

CALORIES

Giver 48

Receiver 48

- ○ Below Average
- ○ Average
- ○ Above Average
- ○ Whoa!

COMMENTS

JANUARY 09)

THE EDGE OF MY SEAT

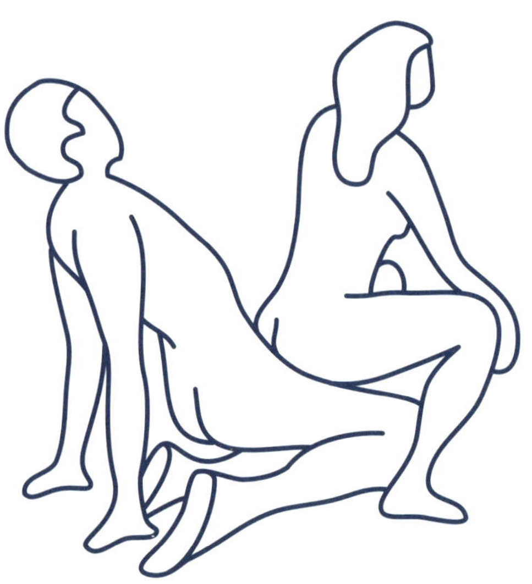

CALORIES

Giver 117.6

Receiver 54

- ○ Below Average
- ○ Average
- ○ Above Average
- ○ Whoa!

COMMENTS

JANUARY 10)

A MOVABLE FEAST

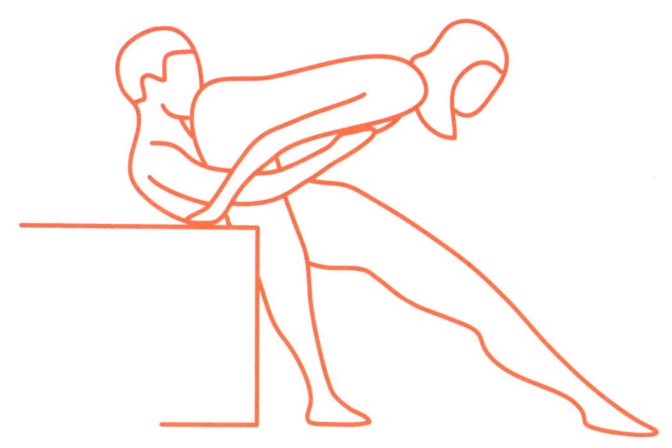

CALORIES		EQUIPMENT
Giver	67.2	Bed
Receiver	48	

- ○ Below Average
- ○ Average
- ○ Above Average
- ○ Whoa!

COMMENTS

JANUARY 11)

THE TWO-HEADED SNAKE

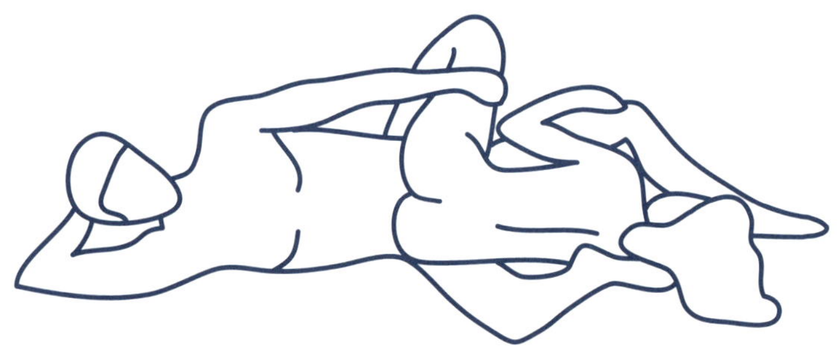

CALORIES

Giver 19

Receiver 54

○ Below Average

○ Average

○ Above Average

○ Whoa!

COMMENTS

JANUARY 12)
"ARE THOSE COLORED CONTACTS?"

CALORIES		EQUIPMENT
Giver	75.6	Bed
Receiver	54	

- ○ Below Average
- ○ Average
- ○ Above Average
- ○ Whoa!

COMMENTS

JANUARY 13)
THE LONG GOODBYE

CALORIES
Giver 75.6
Receiver 54

EQUIPMENT
Tissues

- ○ Below Average
- ○ Average
- ○ Above Average
- ○ Whoa!

COMMENTS

JANUARY 14)
THE FUNKY MONKEY

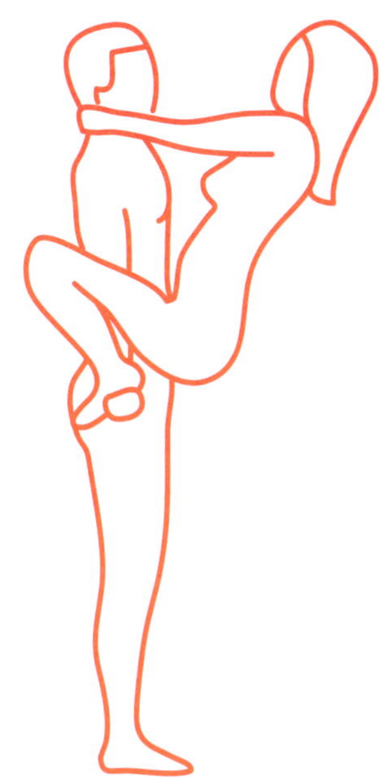

CALORIES		EQUIPMENT
Giver	75.6	Optional:
Receiver	40	Banana

- ○ Below Average
- ○ Average
- ○ Above Average
- ○ Whoa!

COMMENTS

____

____

____

____

____

____

JANUARY 15)
THE FOOT IN MOUTH

CALORIES

Giver 75.6

Receiver 67.2

- ○ Below Average
- ○ Average
- ○ Above Average
- ○ Whoa!

COMMENTS

JANUARY 16)
THE FRAME JOB

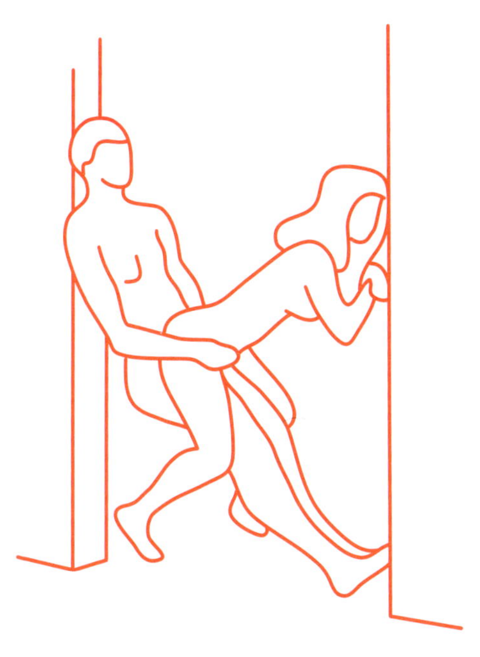

CALORIES

Giver 66

Receiver 75.6

EQUIPMENT

Doorframe

Optional:

Leather Paddle

Nose Guard

- ○ Below Average
- ○ Average
- ○ Above Average
- ○ Whoa!

COMMENTS

___

___

___

___

___

___

JANUARY 17)
STILL LIFE WITH PENETRATION

CALORIES

Giver 19

Receiver 54

- ○ Below Average
- ○ Average
- ○ Above Average
- ○ Whoa!

COMMENTS

JANUARY 18)

THE LAUNCH PAD

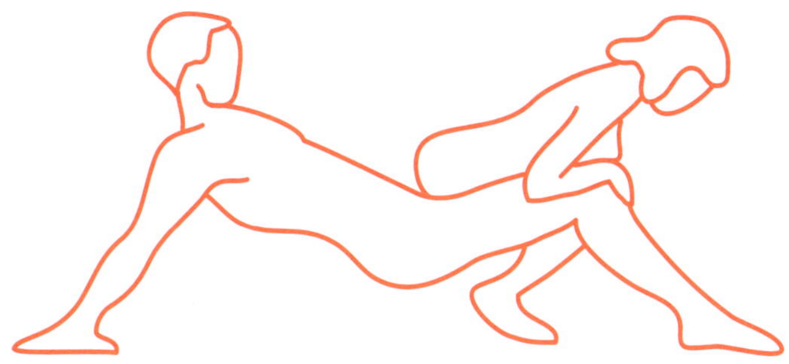

CALORIES

Giver 75.0

Receiver 84

- ○ Below Average
- ○ Average
- ○ Above Average
- ○ Whoa!

COMMENTS

____

____

____

____

____

____

JANUARY 19)
THE MAIN COURSE

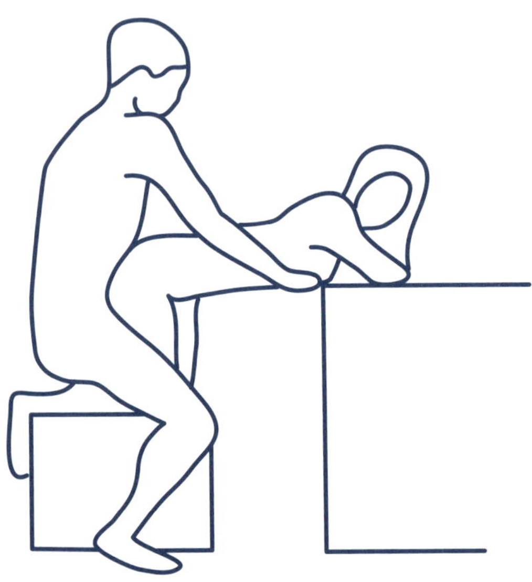

CALORIES		EQUIPMENT
Giver	75.6	Table
Receiver	54	Stool

- ○ Below Average
- ○ Average
- ○ Above Average
- ○ Whoa!

COMMENTS

JANUARY 20)
THE OVER THE HILL

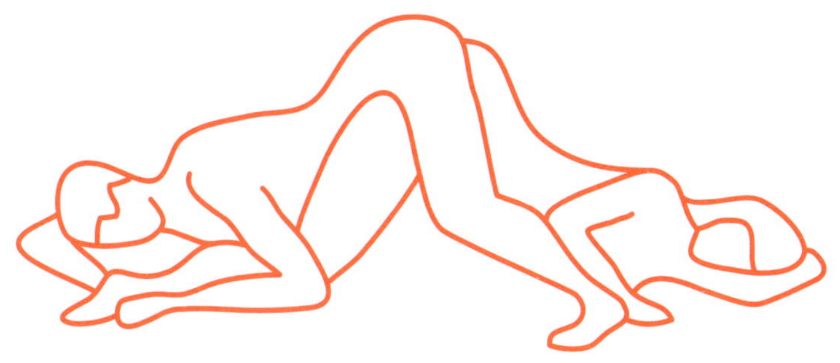

CALORIES

Giver	75.6
Receiver	54

- ○ Below Average
- ○ Average
- ○ Above Average
- ○ Whoa!

COMMENTS

JANUARY 21)
THE PINK FLAMINGO

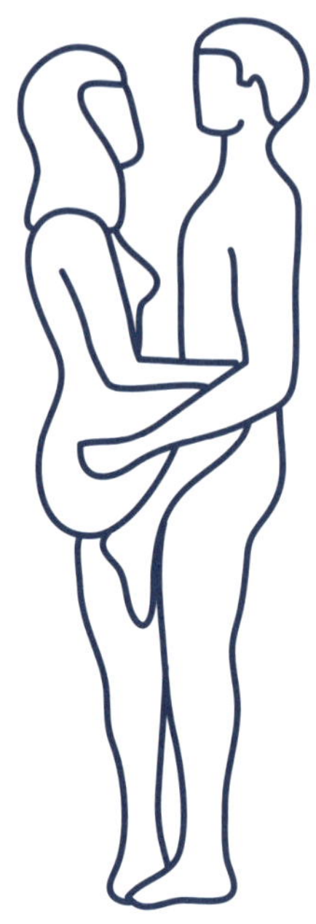

CALORIES

Giver 19

Receiver 26

HAZARD

Leg Cramps

○ Below Average
○ Average
○ Above Average
○ Whoa!

COMMENTS

JANUARY 22)

PULL ME UP, PULL ME DOWN

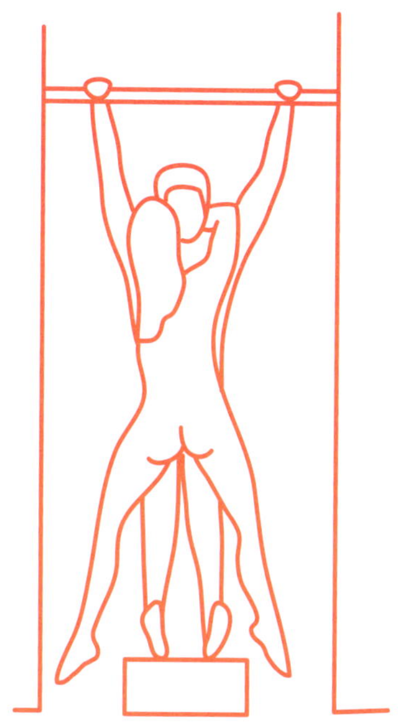

CALORIES		EQUIPMENT	BENEFIT	
Giver	134.4	Pull-Up Bar	Toned Biceps	○ Below Average
Receiver	64	Stool		○ Average
		Deodorant		○ Above Average
				○ Whoa!

COMMENTS

JANUARY 23)

THE LOUNGE LIZARD

CALORIES

Giver 75.6

Receiver 54

EQUIPMENT

Chair

- ○ Below Average
- ○ Average
- ○ Above Average
- ○ Whoa!

COMMENTS

JANUARY 24)

THE BANANA SPLIT

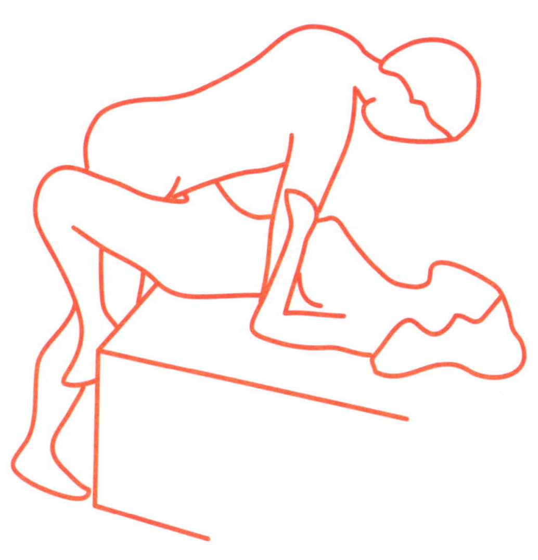

CALORIES

Giver	75.6
Receiver	54

EQUIPMENT

Bed

Whipped Cream

- ○ Below Average
- ○ Average
- ○ Above Average
- ○ Whoa!

COMMENTS

JANUARY 25)

THE COME IN AND SIT DOWN

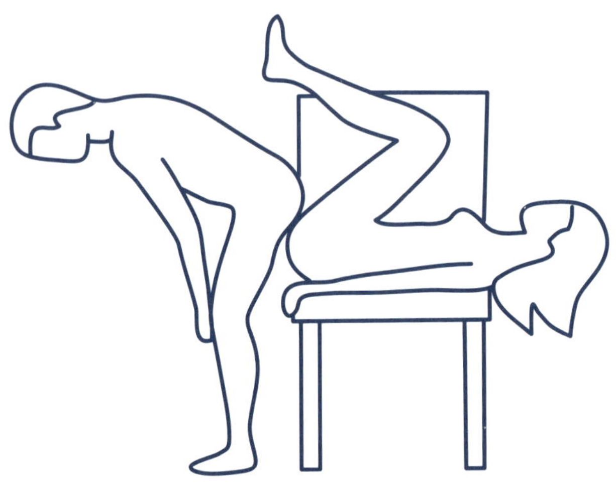

CALORIES

Giver 75.6

Receiver 54

EQUIPMENT

Chair

- ○ Below Average
- ○ Average
- ○ Above Average
- ○ Whoa!

COMMENTS

JANUARY 26)
THE CHEEK TO CHEEK

CALORIES

Giver 19

Receiver 13.6

- ○ Below Average
- ○ Average
- ○ Above Average
- ○ Whoa!

COMMENTS

JANUARY 27)

THE UPSIDE-DOWN CAKE

CALORIES

Giver 100.8

Receiver 72

EQUIPMENT

Wall

- ○ Below Average
- ○ Average
- ○ Above Average
- ○ Whoa!

COMMENTS

JANUARY 28)
THE WINDMILL

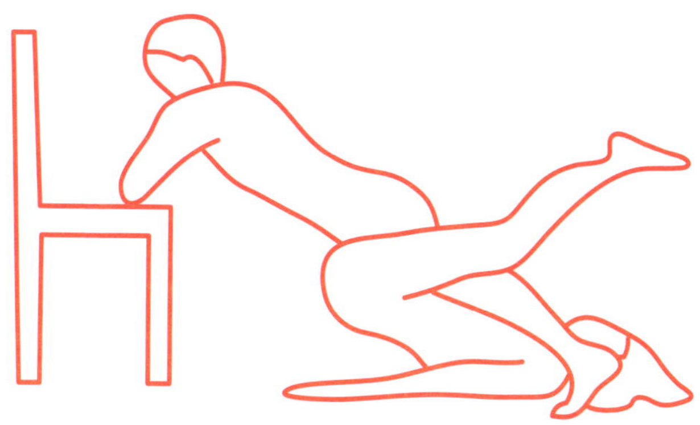

CALORIES

Giver 134.4

Receiver 96

EQUIPMENT

Chair

- ○ Below Average
- ○ Average
- ○ Above Average
- ○ Whoa!

COMMENTS

JANUARY 29)

MINDING THE GAP

CALORIES

Giver	67.2
Receiver	72

EQUIPMENT

Counter

Bed

- ○ Below Average
- ○ Average
- ○ Above Average
- ○ Whoa!

COMMENTS

JANUARY 30)

THE MONKEY SEE, MONKEY DO

CALORIES		EQUIPMENT
Giver	134.4	Pull-Up Bar, Stool, Hand Powder
Receiver	54	Optional: Gorilla Costume

○ Below Average
○ Average
○ Above Average
○ Whoa!

COMMENTS

JANUARY 31)
THE ASSIST

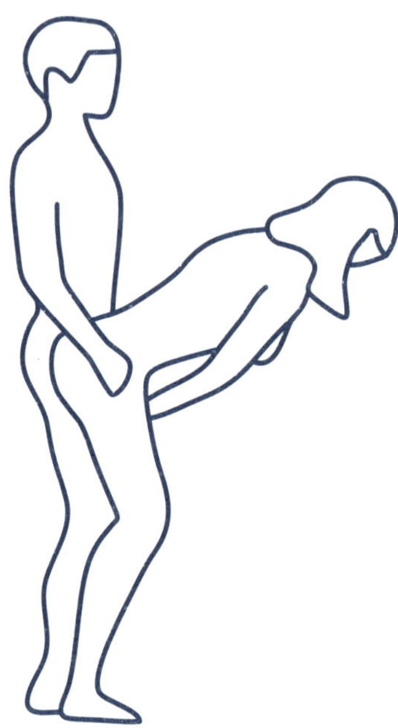

CALORIES

Giver 75.6

Receiver 54

- ○ Below Average
- ○ Average
- ○ Above Average
- ○ Whoa!

COMMENTS

FEBRUARY 01)
THE FINISHING TOUCH

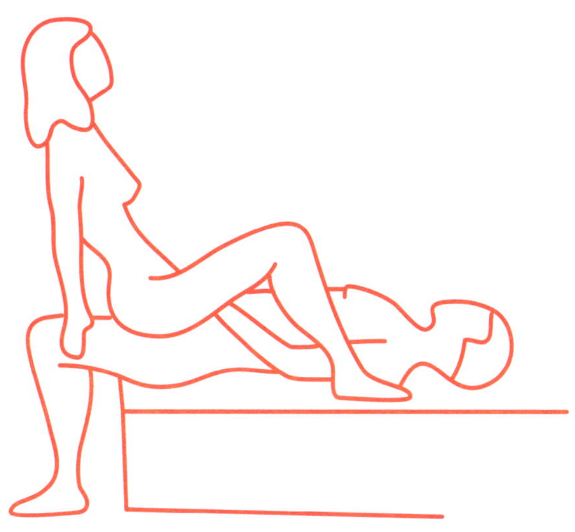

CALORIES		EQUIPMENT
Giver	67.2	Bed
Receiver	54	

- ○ Below Average
- ○ Average
- ○ Above Average
- ○ Whoa!

COMMENTS

____

____

____

____

____

____

FEBRUARY 02)
THE MIDNIGHT SNACK

CALORIES

Giver 54

Receiver 19

EQUIPMENT

Optional: Chocolate Syrup

- ○ Below Average
- ○ Average
- ○ Above Average
- ○ Whoa!

COMMENTS

FEBRUARY 03)

DOWN, BOY!

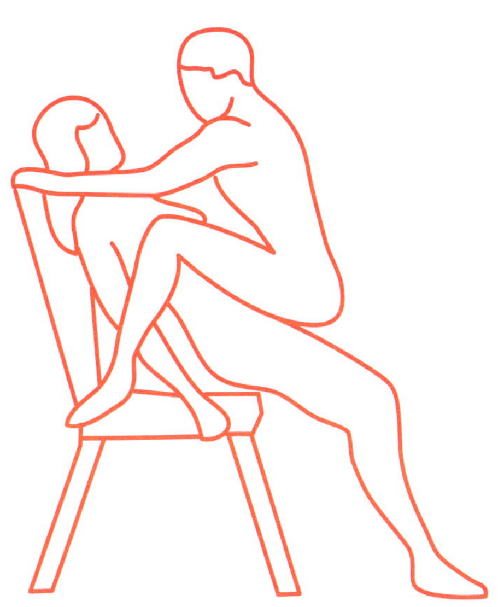

CALORIES

Giver 94

Receiver 65

EQUIPMENT

Leash

- ○ Below Average
- ○ Average
- ○ Above Average
- ○ Whoa!

COMMENTS

FEBRUARY 04)

THE KENTUCKY DERBY

CALORIES		EQUIPMENT	HAZARD	
Giver	134.4	Optional:	Repeatedly Shouting "Giddyap" May Turn Off Some Partners	○ Below Average
Receiver	96	Horsewhip		○ Average
		Riding Cap		○ Above Average
				○ Whoa!

COMMENTS

FEBRUARY 05)
FOOT STUFF

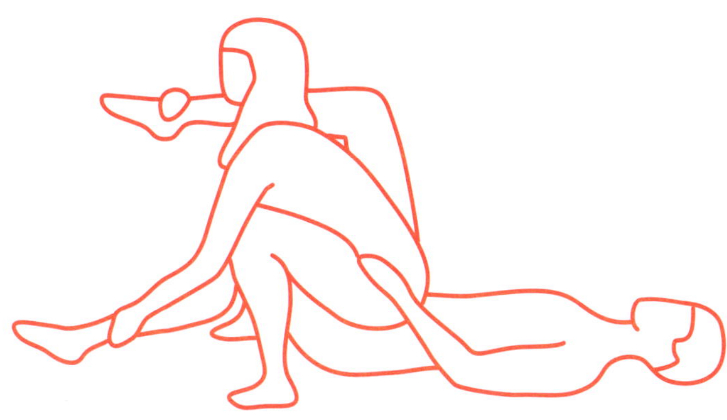

CALORIES

Giver 62

Receiver 49

- ○ Below Average
- ○ Average
- ○ Above Average
- ○ Whoa!

COMMENTS

FEBRUARY 06)
THE FULLBACK

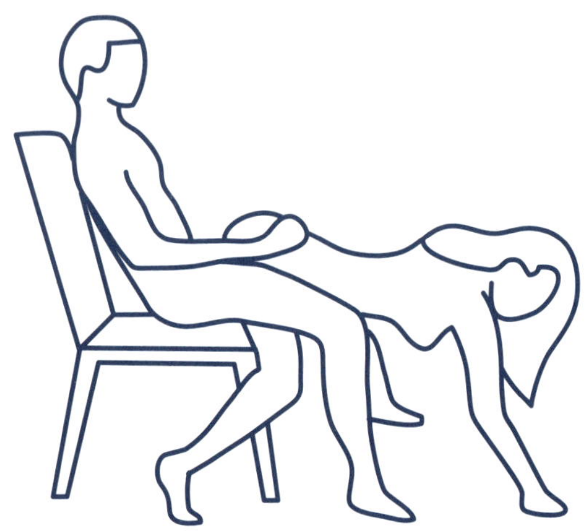

CALORIES
Giver 19
Receiver 48

EQUIPMENT
Chair

- ○ Below Average
- ○ Average
- ○ Above Average
- ○ Whoa!

COMMENTS

FEBRUARY 07)
THE DESK SET

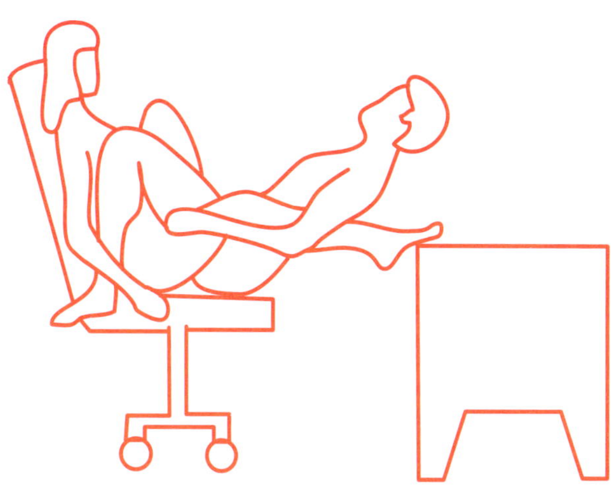

CALORIES		EQUIPMENT
Giver	67.2	Chair
Receiver	48	Desk

- ○ Below Average
- ○ Average
- ○ Above Average
- ○ Whoa!

COMMENTS

FEBRUARY 08)
FALL IN LINE

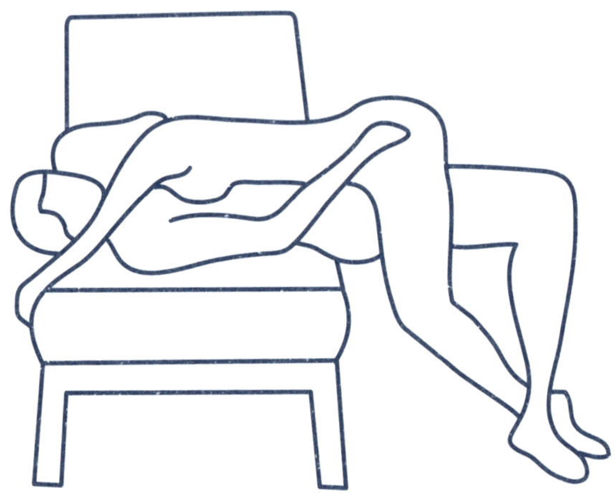

CALORIES
Giver 19
Receiver 48

EQUIPMENT
Chair

- ○ Below Average
- ○ Average
- ○ Above Average
- ○ Whoa!

COMMENTS

FEBRUARY 09)
THE DUMPTRUCK

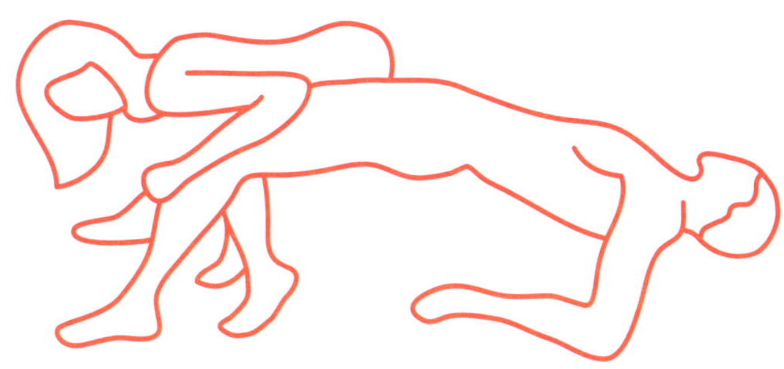

CALORIES

Giver 66

Receiver 38

- ○ Below Average
- ○ Average
- ○ Above Average
- ○ Whoa!

COMMENTS

____

____

____

____

____

____

FEBRUARY 10)

THE "I THINK I'M STUCK"

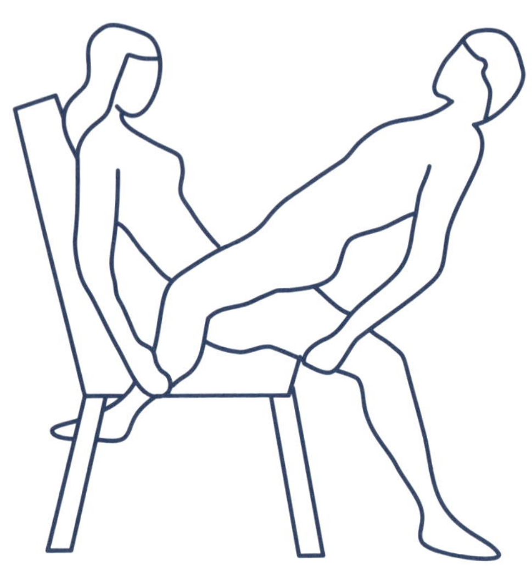

CALORIES

Giver 59

Receiver 46

EQUIPMENT

Chair

- ○ Below Average
- ○ Average
- ○ Above Average
- ○ Whoa!

COMMENTS

FEBRUARY 11)

THE MULTITASKER

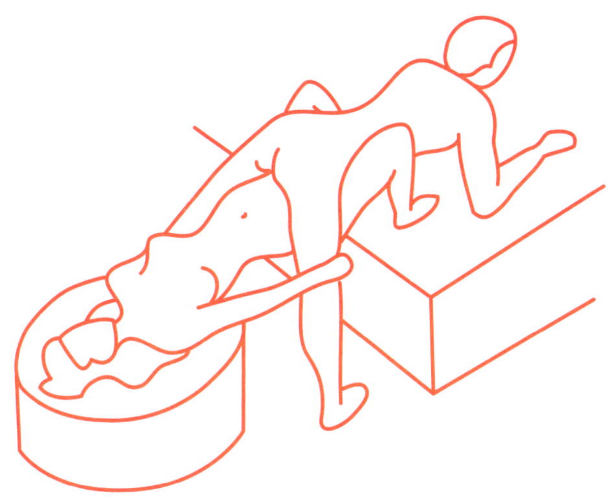

CALORIES

Giver	75.6
Receiver	48

EQUIPMENT

Bed
Ottoman

- ○ Below Average
- ○ Average
- ○ Above Average
- ○ Whoa!

COMMENTS

FEBRUARY 12)

THE EDWARD SCISSORLEGS

CALORIES

Giver 56

Receiver 78

EQUIPMENT

Bed

- ○ Below Average
- ○ Average
- ○ Above Average
- ○ Whoa!

COMMENTS

FEBRUARY 13)
THE STRICTLY BALLROOM

CALORIES
Giver 117.0
Receiver 96

EQUIPMENT
High Heels
Dance Music

- ○ Below Average
- ○ Average
- ○ Above Average
- ○ Whoa!

COMMENTS

FEBRUARY 14)

THE VERY HAPPY VALENTINE'S DAY

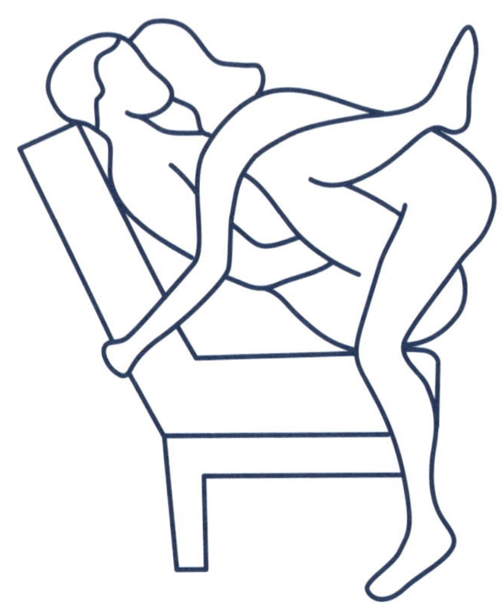

CALORIES		EQUIPMENT	BENEFIT	
Giver	83	Chair	True Love	○ Below Average
Receiver	91	Flowers		○ Average
		Chocolates		○ Above Average
				○ Whoa!

COMMENTS

FEBRUARY 15)
SADDLE UP

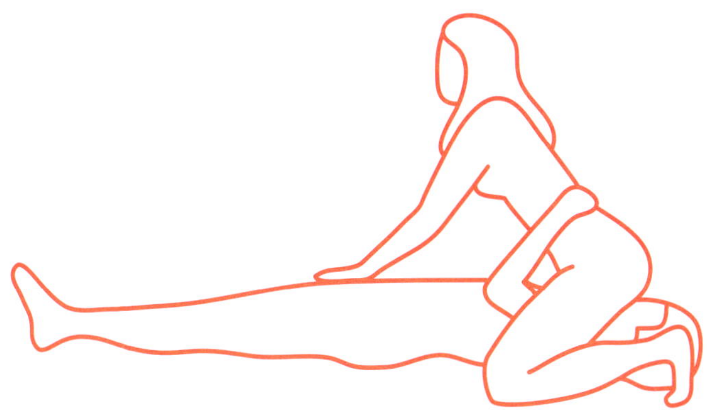

CALORIES

Giver 19

Receiver 48

- ○ Below Average
- ○ Average
- ○ Above Average
- ○ Whoa!

COMMENTS

FEBRUARY 16)
THE NOW WHAT?

CALORIES
Giver 75.6
Receiver 48

EQUIPMENT
Rocking Chair

- ○ Below Average
- ○ Average
- ○ Above Average
- ○ Whoa!

COMMENTS

FEBRUARY 17)
THE UNBEARABLE LIGHTNESS OF SCREWING

CALORIES

Giver	100.0
Receiver	132

- ○ Below Average
- ○ Average
- ○ Above Average
- ○ Whoa!

COMMENTS

FEBRUARY 18)

BRINGING UP THE REAR

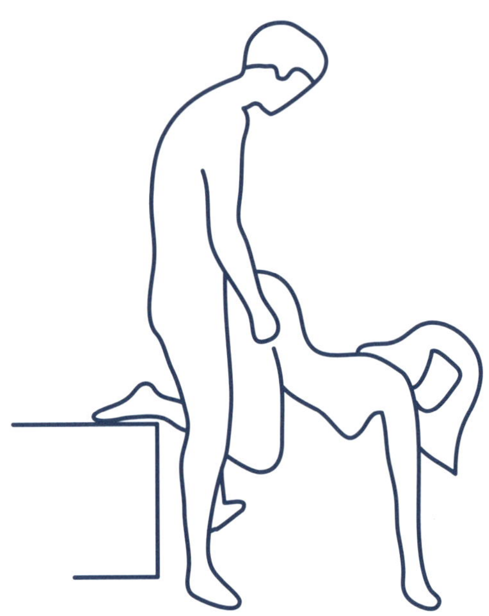

CALORIES

Giver 75.6

Receiver 54

EQUIPMENT

Bed

- ○ Below Average
- ○ Average
- ○ Above Average
- ○ Whoa!

COMMENTS

FEBRUARY 19)
THE LOVE SEAT

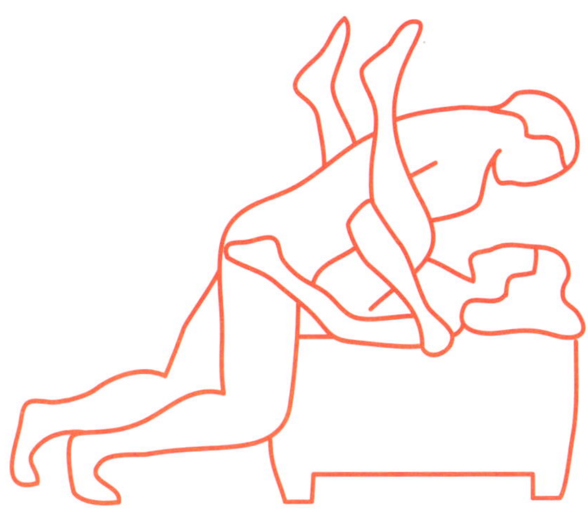

CALORIES

Giver 76.0

Receiver 54

EQUIPMENT

Ottoman

- ○ Below Average
- ○ Average
- ○ Above Average
- ○ Whoa!

COMMENTS

____

____

____

____

____

____

FEBRUARY 20)
THE SIDECAR

CALORIES

Giver 67.2

Receiver 54

EQUIPMENT

Rocking Chair

- ○ Below Average
- ○ Average
- ○ Above Average
- ○ Whoa!

COMMENTS

FEBRUARY 21)
THE BACKPEDALER

CALORIES		EQUIPMENT
Giver	67.2	Chair
Receiver	54	

- ○ Below Average
- ○ Average
- ○ Above Average
- ○ Whoa!

COMMENTS

FEBRUARY 22)
THE SWAN BOAT

CALORIES

Giver 19

Receiver 96

EQUIPMENT

Bed

- ○ Below Average
- ○ Average
- ○ Above Average
- ○ Whoa!

COMMENTS

FEBRUARY 23)

THE OVERZEALOUS CONGRATULATIONS

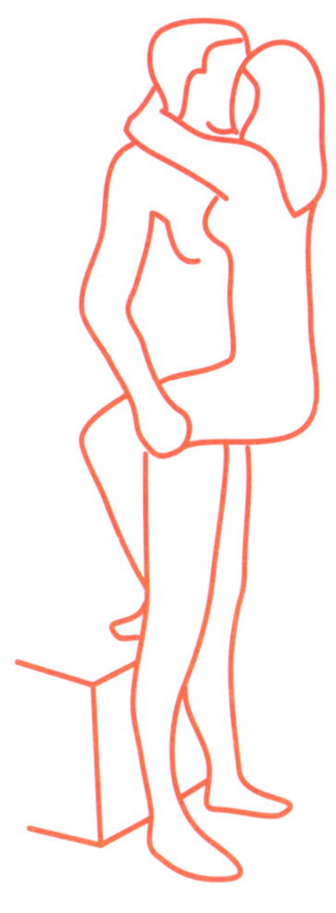

CALORIES

Giver 85

Receiver 43

EQUIPMENT

Stool

- ○ Below Average
- ○ Average
- ○ Above Average
- ○ Whoa!

COMMENTS

FEBRUARY 24)
THE OLD TOWN RODE

CALORIES

Giver 168

Receiver 48

- ○ Below Average
- ○ Average
- ○ Above Average
- ○ Whoa!

COMMENTS

FEBRUARY 25)
THE ADULT SHOW AND TELL

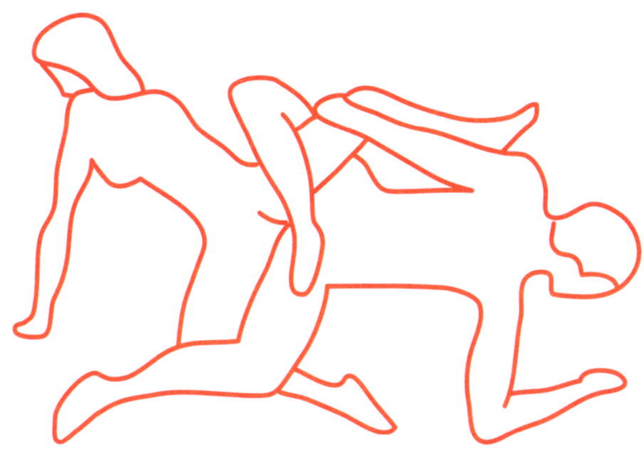

CALORIES

Giver 70

Receiver 61

- ○ Below Average
- ○ Average
- ○ Above Average
- ○ Whoa!

COMMENTS

FEBRUARY 26)
THE CARRIED AWAY

CALORIES		**EQUIPMENT**
Giver	50.4	Rocking Chair
Receiver	96	

- ○ Below Average
- ○ Average
- ○ Above Average
- ○ Whoa!

COMMENTS

FEBRUARY 27)
THE ROCK STEADY

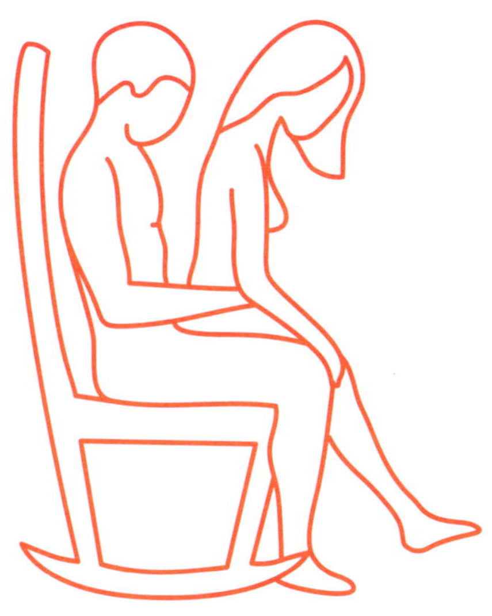

CALORIES

Giver 19

Receiver 54

EQUIPMENT

Rocking Chair

- ○ Below Average
- ○ Average
- ○ Above Average
- ○ Whoa!

COMMENTS

FEBRUARY 28)
THE NO ELBOWS ON THE TABLE

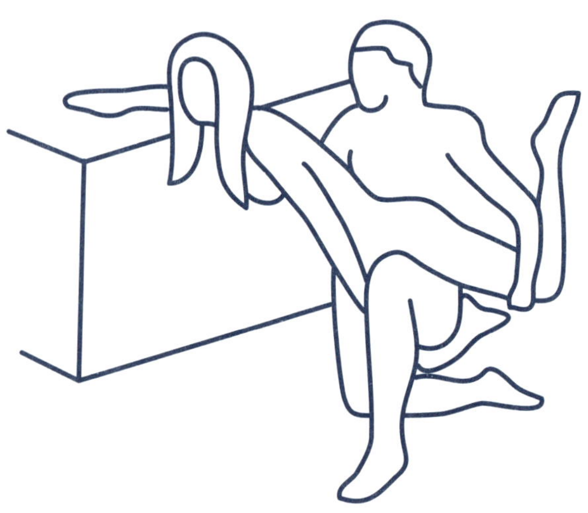

CALORIES

Giver	75.6
Receiver	48

EQUIPMENT

Table

- ○ Below Average
- ○ Average
- ○ Above Average
- ○ Whoa!

COMMENTS

MARCH 01)
THE LOW

CALORIES

Giver	66
Receiver	66

- O Below Average
- O Average
- O Above Average
- O Whoa!

COMMENTS

MARCH 02)
CLIMBING THE STAIRS

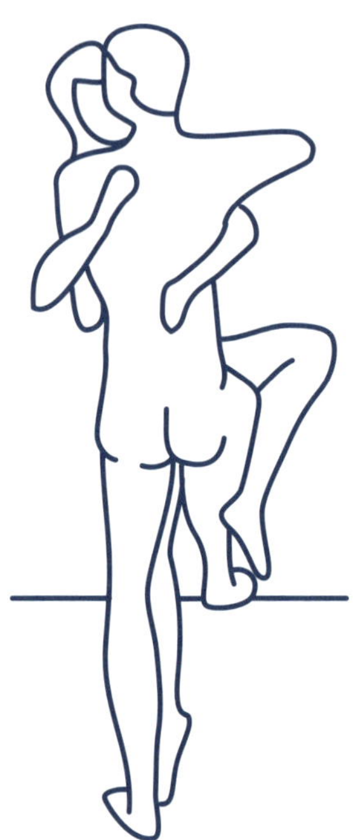

CALORIES
Giver 61
Receiver 70

EQUIPMENT
Stair

- ○ Below Average
- ○ Average
- ○ Above Average
- ○ Whoa!

COMMENTS

MARCH 03)
THE STARGAZER

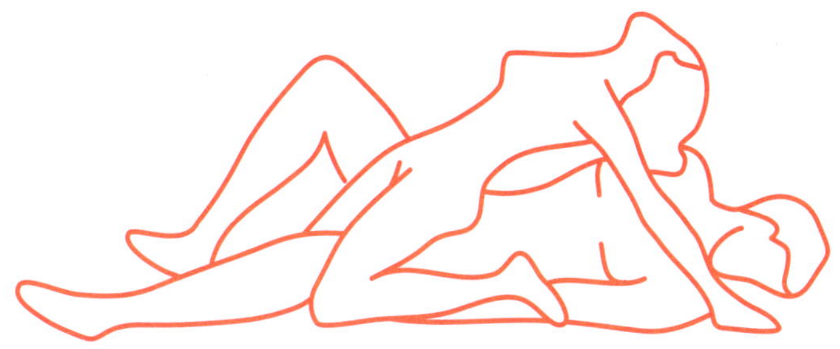

CALORIES

Giver	67.2
Receiver	96

HAZARD

Cloudy Nights

○ Below Average
○ Average
○ Above Average
○ Whoa!

COMMENTS

MARCH 04)
THE TWO TO TANGO

CALORIES

Giver 75.6

Receiver 54

- ○ Below Average
- ○ Average
- ○ Above Average
- ○ Whoa!

COMMENTS

MARCH 05)

THE SWING FLING

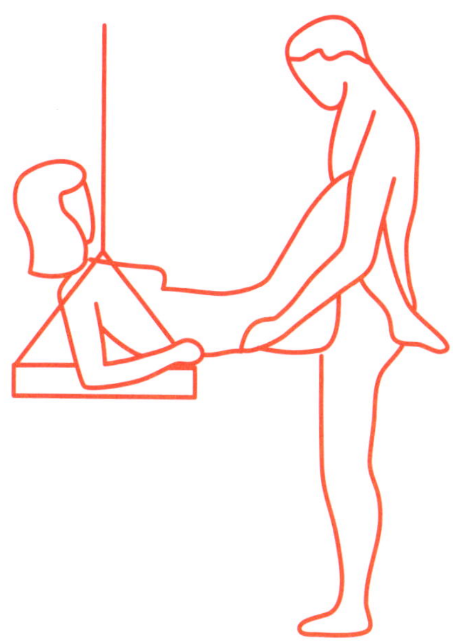

CALORIES

Giver 75.6

Receiver 66

EQUIPMENT

Porch Swing

- ○ Below Average
- ○ Average
- ○ Above Average
- ○ Whoa!

COMMENTS

MARCH 06)

CROSSING THE LINE

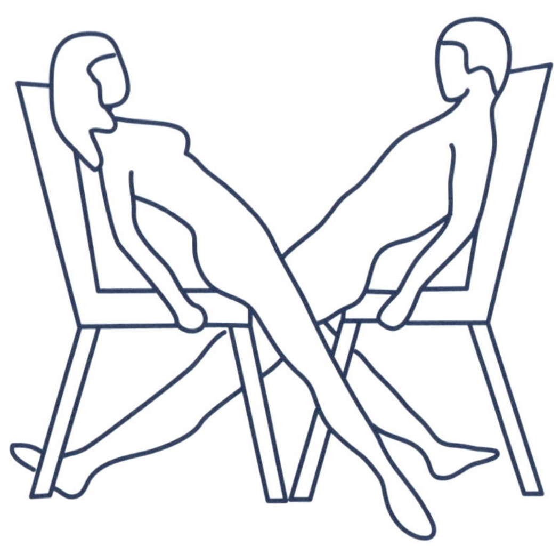

CALORIES

Giver 56

Receiver 61

EQUIPMENT

Two Chairs

- ○ Below Average
- ○ Average
- ○ Above Average
- ○ Whoa!

COMMENTS

MARCH 07)
THE ROCKET

CALORIES
Giver 75.6
Receiver 96

EQUIPMENT
Rocking Chair

- ○ Below Average
- ○ Average
- ○ Above Average
- ○ Whoa!

COMMENTS

MARCH 08)
THE WHEELBARROW RACE

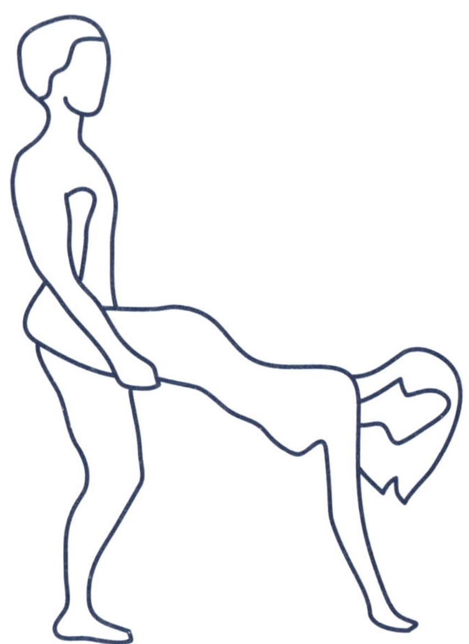

CALORIES

Giver 100.8

Receiver 96

- ○ Below Average
- ○ Average
- ○ Above Average
- ○ Whoa!

COMMENTS

MARCH 09)
THE BUM DEAL

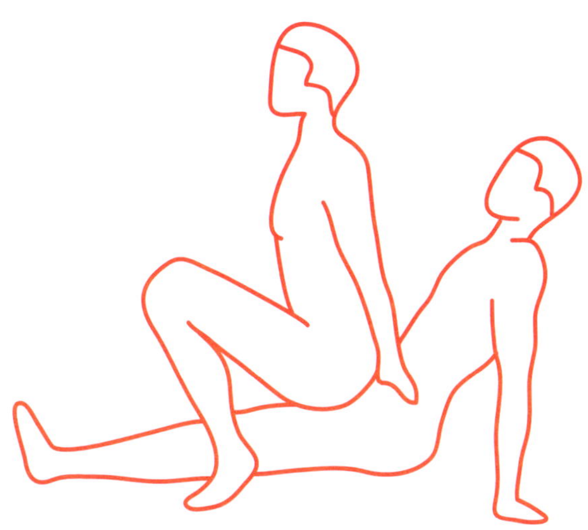

CALORIES

Giver	75.6
Receiver	75.6

- ○ Below Average
- ○ Average
- ○ Above Average
- ○ Whoa!

COMMENTS

____

____

____

____

____

____

MARCH 10)
PACKING THE SUITCASE

CALORIES

Giver 117.6

Receiver 48

EQUIPMENT

Bed

- ○ Below Average
- ○ Average
- ○ Above Average
- ○ Whoa!

COMMENTS

MARCH 11)
ASSEMBLY REQUIRED

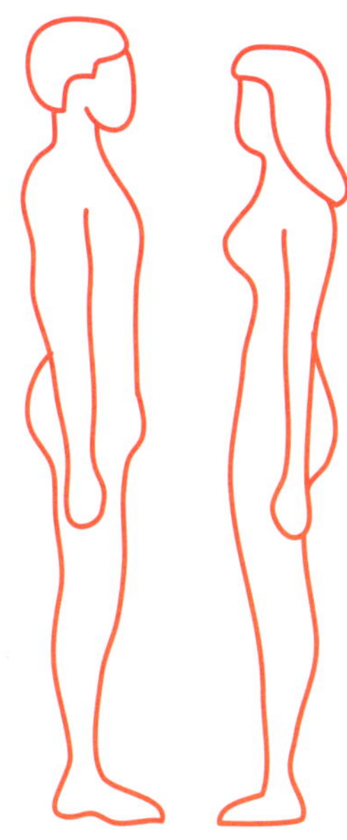

CALORIES
Giver 19
Receiver 13.6

HAZARD
Intense Frustration

- ○ Below Average
- ○ Average
- ○ Above Average
- ○ Whoa!

COMMENTS

MARCH 12)
THE WALLFLOWER

CALORIES

Giver 117.6

Receiver 84

- ○ Below Average
- ○ Average
- ○ Above Average
- ○ Whoa!

COMMENTS

MARCH 13)

LIKE BUTTER

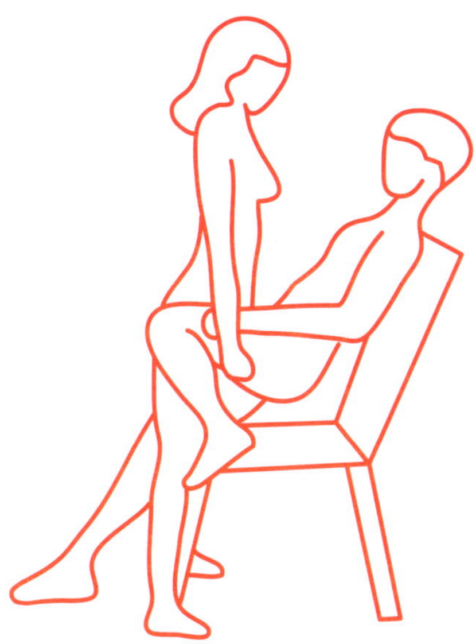

CALORIES

Giver	55
Receiver	60

EQUIPMENT

Chair

- ○ Below Average
- ○ Average
- ○ Above Average
- ○ Whoa!

COMMENTS

____

____

____

____

____

____

MARCH 14)
DINNER IS SERVED

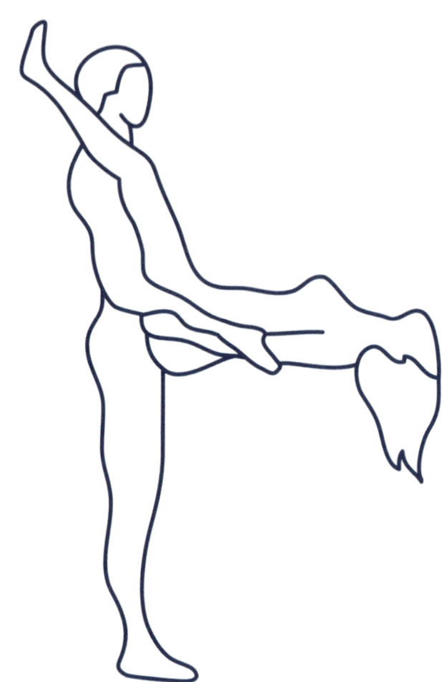

CALORIES

Giver 100.8

Receiver 96

- ○ Below Average
- ○ Average
- ○ Above Average
- ○ Whoa!

COMMENTS

MARCH 15)

THE HEART OPENER

CALORIES

Giver 134.4

Receiver 72

- ○ Below Average
- ○ Average
- ○ Above Average
- ○ Whoa!

COMMENTS

MARCH 16)

THE FEEDING TROUGH

CALORIES

Giver 75.6

Receiver 96

- ○ Below Average
- ○ Average
- ○ Above Average
- ○ Whoa!

COMMENTS

MARCH 17)

THE OUT-OF-TOWN GUESTS

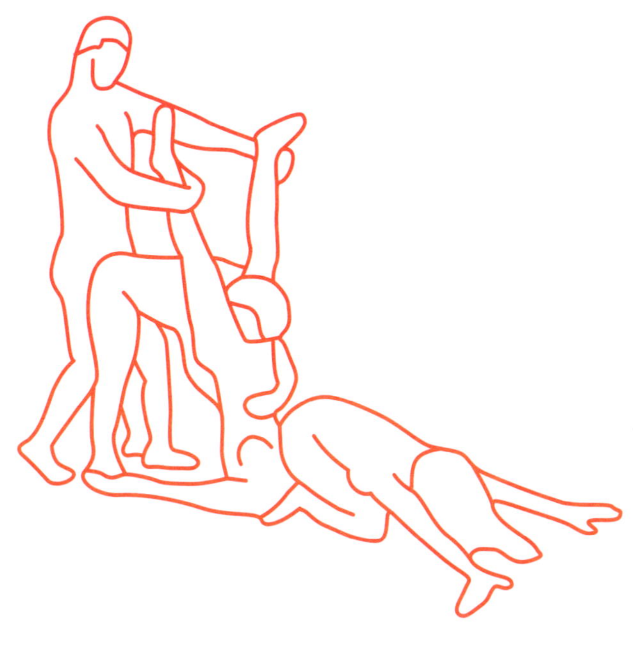

CALORIES

Giver	80
Giver/Receiver	88.4
Giver/Receiver	93
Receiver	54

BENEFIT

No Need for Guest Bedroom

- ○ Below Average
- ○ Average
- ○ Above Average
- ○ Whoa!

COMMENTS

MARCH 18)
THE LEG HUG

CALORIES

Giver	75.6
Receiver	96

HAZARD

Rug Burn

- ○ Below Average
- ○ Average
- ○ Above Average
- ○ Whoa!

COMMENTS

MARCH 19)
THE BUNNY SLOPE

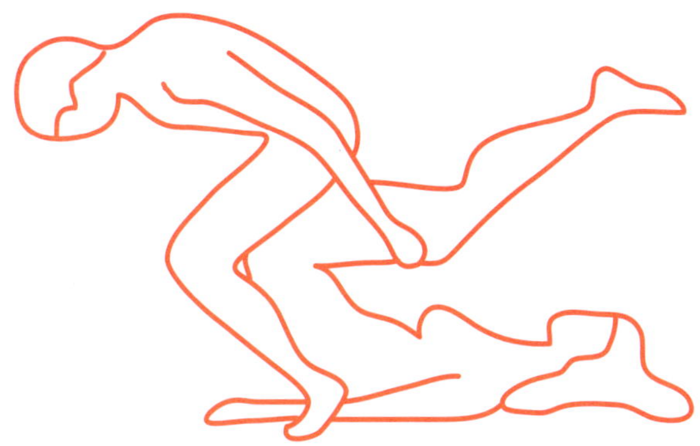

CALORIES

Giver 92.4

Receiver 48

EQUIPMENT

Ski Poles

- ○ Below Average
- ○ Average
- ○ Above Average
- ○ Whoa!

COMMENTS

MARCH 20)
THE WAP

CALORIES

Giver 19

Receiver 54

- ○ Below Average
- ○ Average
- ○ Above Average
- ○ Whoa!

COMMENTS

MARCH 21)

THE TWIST AND SHOUT

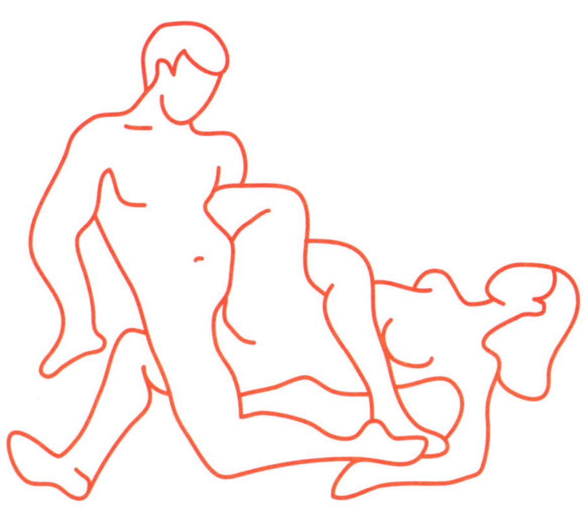

CALORIES

Giver 101.4

Receiver 96

HAZARD

Getting Stuck

- ○ Below Average
- ○ Average
- ○ Above Average
- ○ Whoa!

COMMENTS

MARCH 22)
THE PERPENDICULAR

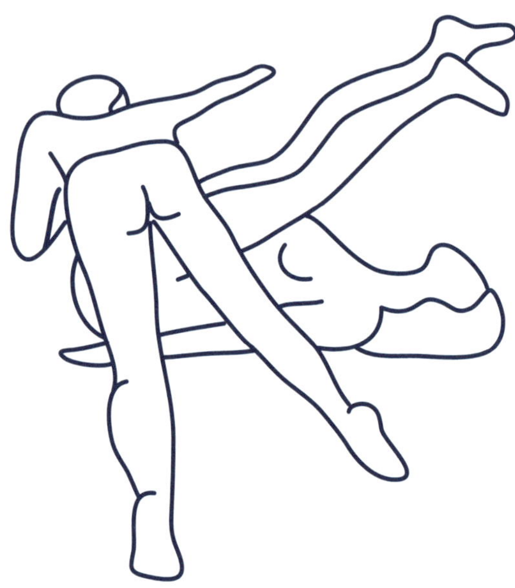

CALORIES

Giver 75.6

Receiver 48

- ○ Below Average
- ○ Average
- ○ Above Average
- ○ Whoa!

COMMENTS

MARCH 23)
THE OVER AND OVER

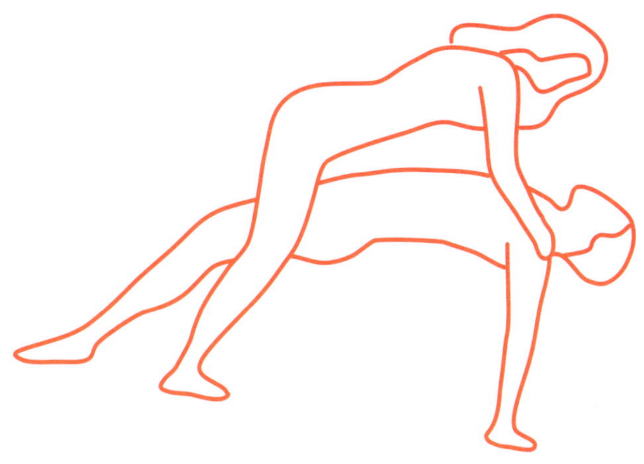

CALORIES

Giver	134.4
Receiver	95

- ○ Below Average
- ○ Average
- ○ Above Average
- ○ Whoa!

COMMENTS

MARCH 24)
THE FRIENDLY ASSASSIN

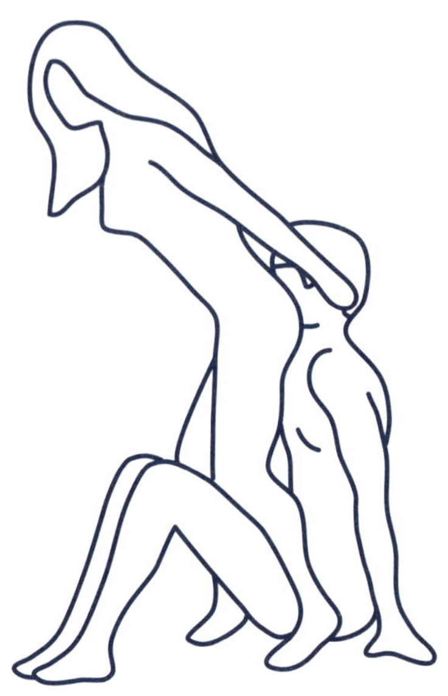

CALORIES

Giver 19

Receiver 54

- ○ Below Average
- ○ Average
- ○ Above Average
- ○ Whoa!

COMMENTS

MARCH 25)
THE WHEN IN DOUBT

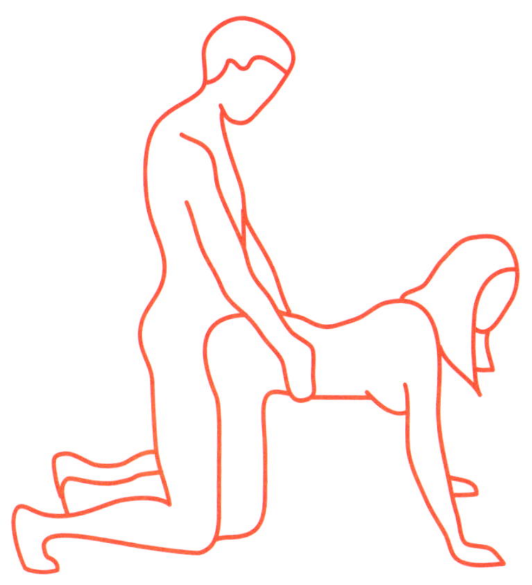

CALORIES		EQUIPMENT	HAZARD
Giver	75.6	Optional:	Boredom
Receiver	54	Spiked Collar	

- ○ Below Average
- ○ Average
- ○ Above Average
- ○ Whoa!

COMMENTS

______

______

______

______

______

______

MARCH 26)

THE LOW PROFILE

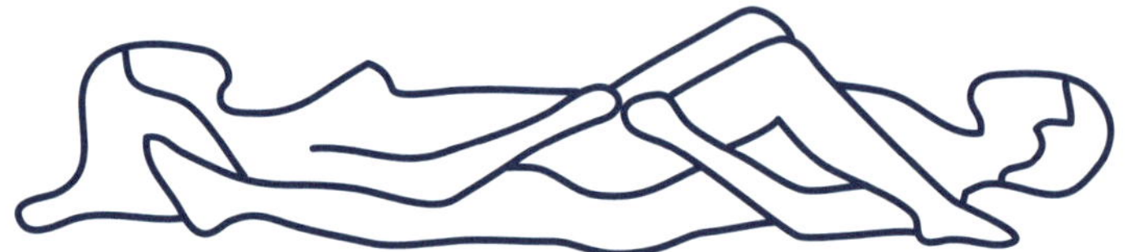

CALORIES

Giver 19

Receiver 13.6

HAZARD

Falling Asleep

- ○ Below Average
- ○ Average
- ○ Above Average
- ○ Whoa!

COMMENTS

MARCH 27)

THE NIP AND TUCK

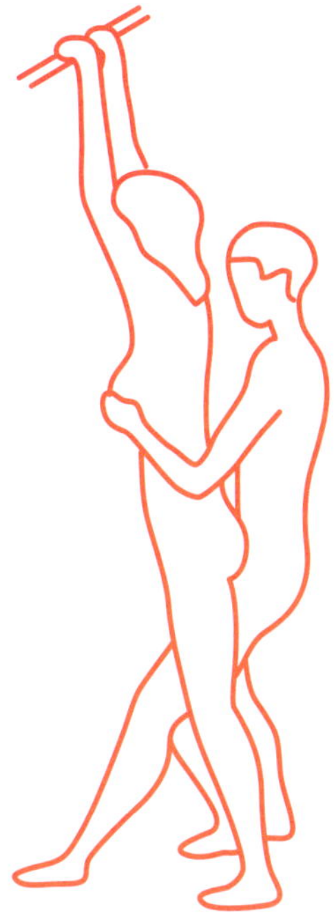

CALORIES

Giver 75.6

Receiver 66

EQUIPMENT

Pull Up Bar

- ○ Below Average
- ○ Average
- ○ Above Average
- ○ Whoa!

COMMENTS

____

____

____

____

____

____

MARCH 28)

THE TWIST ENDING

CALORIES

Giver 75.6

Receiver 48

EQUIPMENT

Rocking Chair

- ○ Below Average
- ○ Average
- ○ Above Average
- ○ Whoa!

COMMENTS

MARCH 29)
THE DEEP TALK

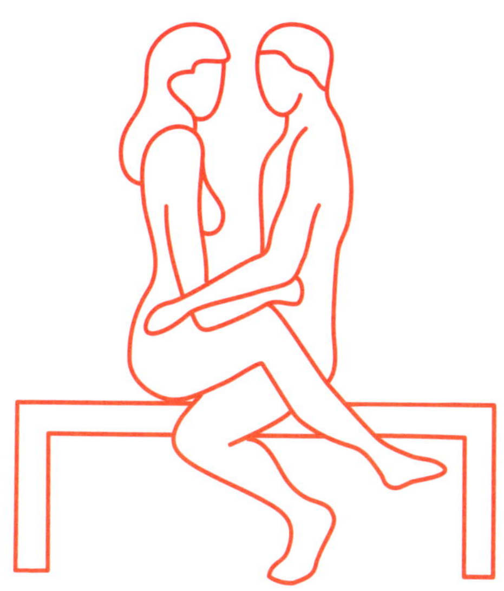

CALORIES		EQUIPMENT
Giver	19	Hanky
Receiver	13.6	Table

- ○ Below Average
- ○ Average
- ○ Above Average
- ○ Whoa!

COMMENTS

MARCH 30)
THE REVERSE WHEELBARROW

CALORIES

Giver 100.8

Receiver 96

- ○ Below Average
- ○ Average
- ○ Above Average
- ○ Whoa!

COMMENTS

MARCH 31)
THE HOBBYHORSE

CALORIES

Giver 117.6

Receiver 120

EQUIPMENT

Rocking Chair

- ○ Below Average
- ○ Average
- ○ Above Average
- ○ Whoa!

COMMENTS

APRIL 01)

APRIL FOOL'S PARADISE

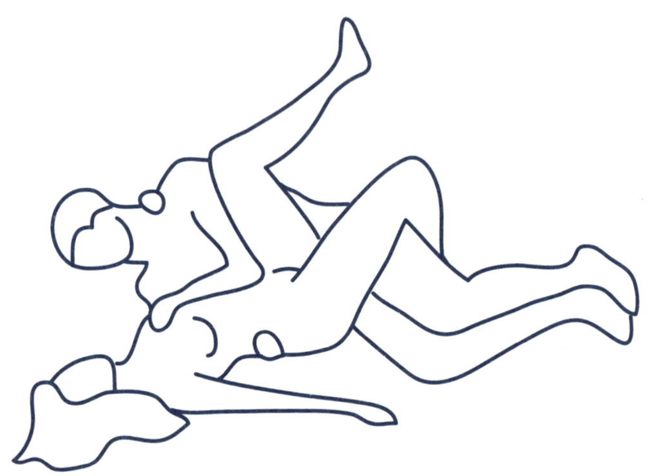

CALORIES

Giver 75.6

Receiver 54

- ○ Below Average
- ○ Average
- ○ Above Average
- ○ Whoa!

COMMENTS

APRIL 02)

IT'S A WRAP

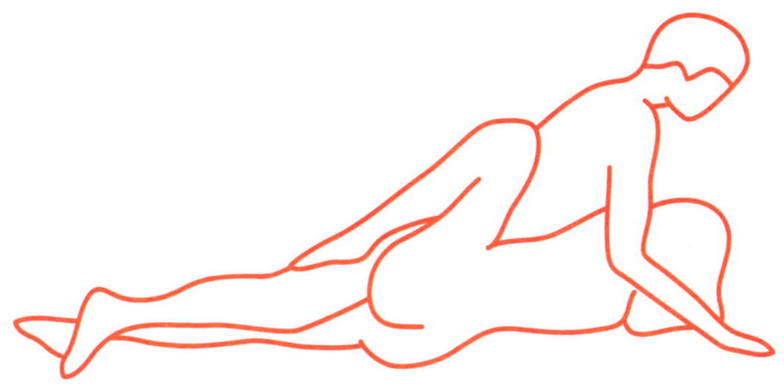

CALORIES

Giver 75.6

Receiver 48

○ Below Average

○ Average

○ Above Average

○ Whoa!

COMMENTS

____

____

____

____

____

____

APRIL 03)
THE BLOCKING SLED

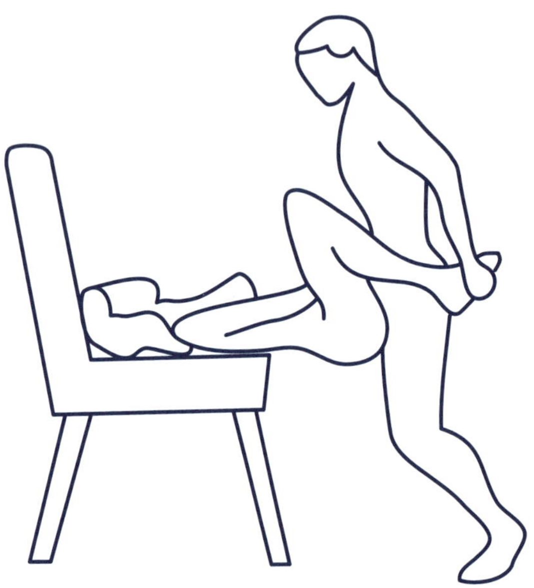

CALORIES

Giver 75.6

Receiver 59

EQUIPMENT

Chair

- ○ Below Average
- ○ Average
- ○ Above Average
- ○ Whoa!

COMMENTS

APRIL 04)

THE NIGHT CRAWLER

CALORIES

Giver 67.2

Receiver 48

○ Below Average

○ Average

○ Above Average

○ Whoa!

COMMENTS

APRIL 05)

THE DOWN AND DIRTY

CALORIES

Giver 75.6

Receiver 48

EQUIPMENT

Bed

- ○ Below Average
- ○ Average
- ○ Above Average
- ○ Whoa!

COMMENTS

APRIL 06)
THE RINGSIDE SEAT

CALORIES		BENEFIT
Giver	75.6	Doing Up Close
Receiver	13.6	

- ○ Below Average
- ○ Average
- ○ Above Average
- ○ Whoa!

COMMENTS

APRIL 07)

THE HOLD ON

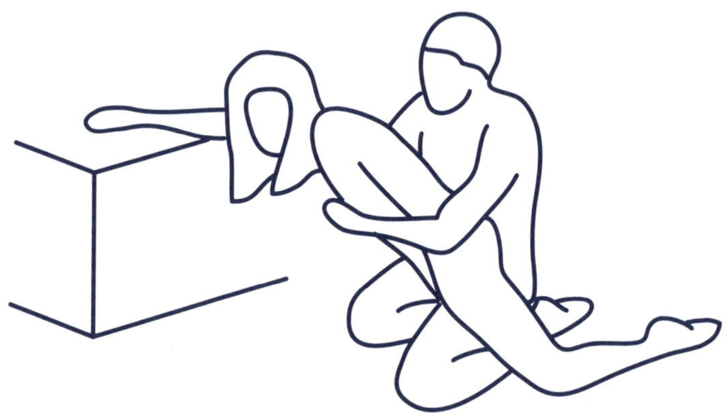

CALORIES

Giver 75.6

Receiver 48

EQUIPMENT

Bed

- ○ Below Average
- ○ Average
- ○ Above Average
- ○ Whoa!

COMMENTS

APRIL 08)

THE JAM SESSION

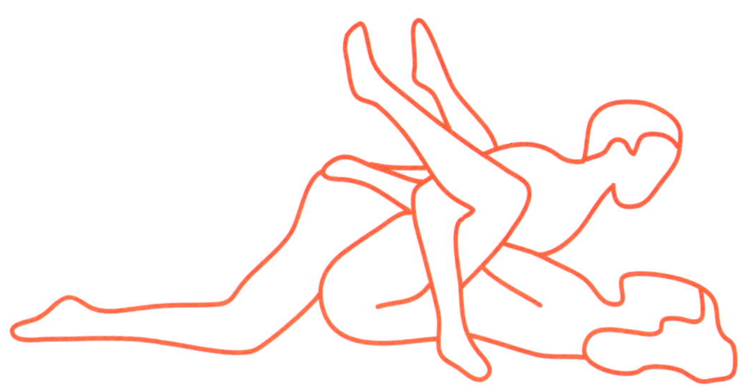

CALORIES

Giver 75.6

Receiver 54

HAZARD

Heavy Breathing

○ Below Average

○ Average

○ Above Average

○ Whoa!

COMMENTS

APRIL 09)
BROOKLYN SIX-NINE

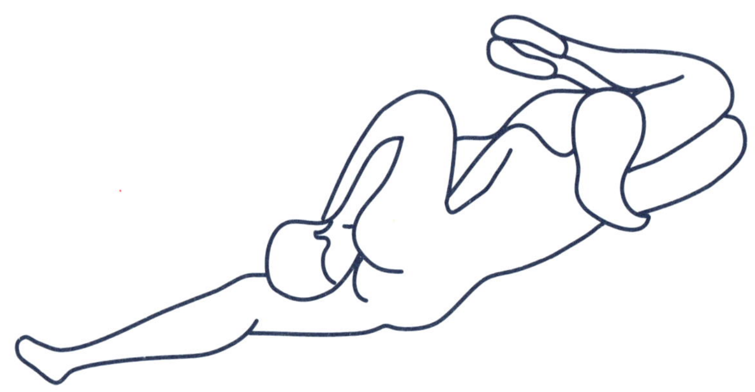

CALORIES

Giver 67.2

Receiver 48

- ○ Below Average
- ○ Average
- ○ Above Average
- ○ Whoa!

COMMENTS

APRIL 10)
ROLL PLAY

CALORIES

Giver 75.6

Receiver 96

EQUIPMENT

Enormous Pipe

- ○ Below Average
- ○ Average
- ○ Above Average
- ○ Whoa!

COMMENTS

APRIL 11)

THE "I'LL BE RIGHT BACK"

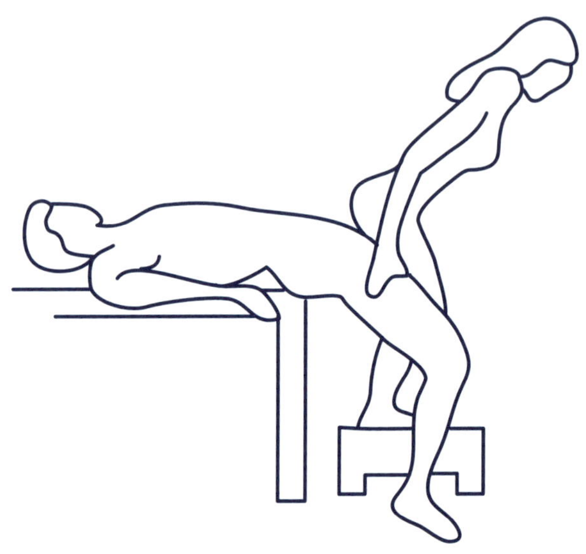

CALORIES

Giver 19

Receiver 120

EQUIPMENT

Table

Stool

- ○ Below Average
- ○ Average
- ○ Above Average
- ○ Whoa!

COMMENTS

APRIL 12)

THE RISING TIDE

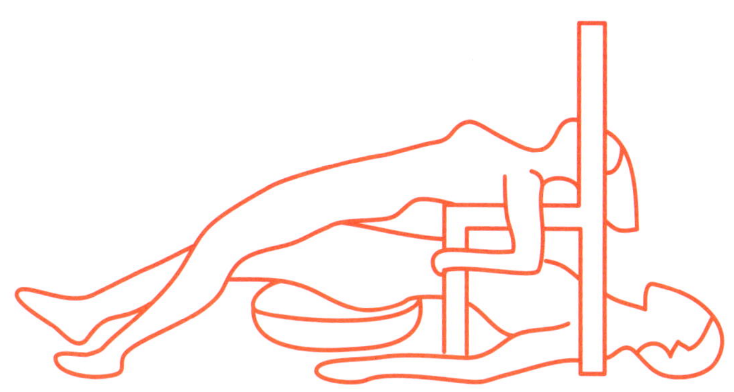

CALORIES

Giver 19

Receiver 48

EQUIPMENT

Chair

Pillow

- ○ Below Average
- ○ Average
- ○ Above Average
- ○ Whoa!

COMMENTS

____

____

____

____

____

____

APRIL 13)
THE REAR-ENDER

CALORIES

Giver 75.6

Receiver 54

EQUIPMENT

Chair

- ○ Below Average
- ○ Average
- ○ Above Average
- ○ Whoa!

COMMENTS

APRIL 14)
THE BACKSWING

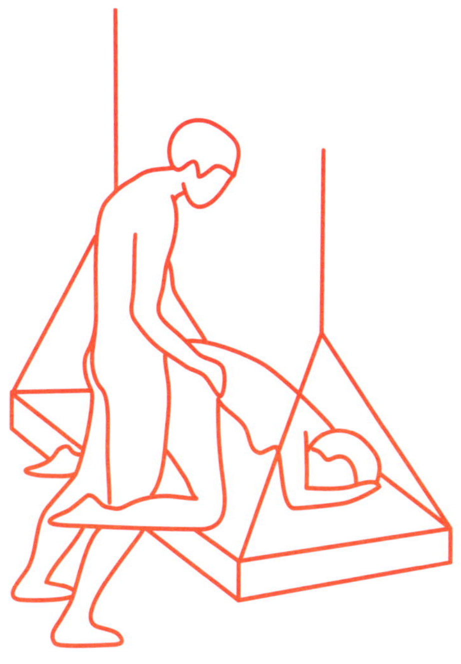

CALORIES

Giver 75.6

Receiver 66

EQUIPMENT

Porch Swing

- ○ Below Average
- ○ Average
- ○ Above Average
- ○ Whoa!

COMMENTS

APRIL 15)

SIMON SAYS, "LAY DOWN WITH YOUR HEAD UNDER THE CHAIR"

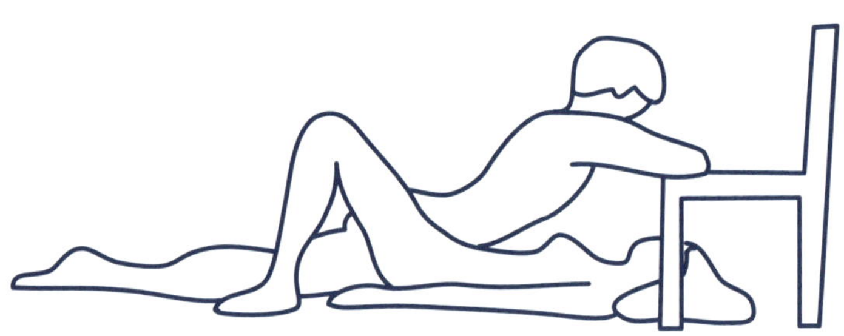

CALORIES

Giver 75.6

Receiver 54

EQUIPMENT

Chair

HAZARD

Listening to Everything Simon Says

- ○ Below Average
- ○ Average
- ○ Above Average
- ○ Whoa!

COMMENTS

APRIL 16)
THE HANGNAIL

CALORIES

Giver 67.2

Receiver 96

- ○ Below Average
- ○ Average
- ○ Above Average
- ○ Whoa!

COMMENTS

APRIL 17)
THE HANG IN THERE

CALORIES

Giver 134.4

Receiver 96

- ○ Below Average
- ○ Average
- ○ Above Average
- ○ Whoa!

COMMENTS

APRIL 18)
THE TWIDDLE

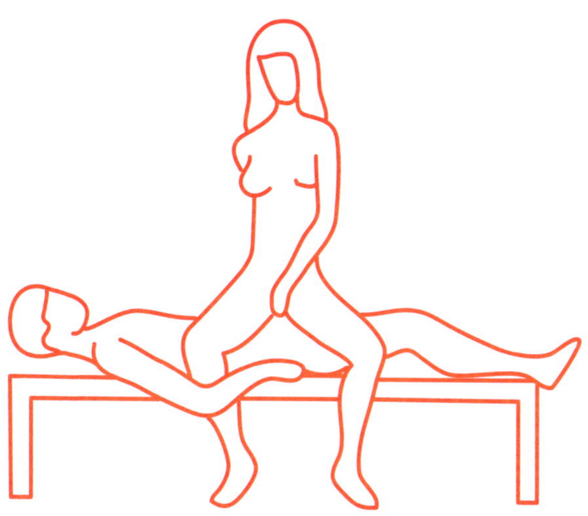

CALORIES
Giver 19
Receiver 54

EQUIPMENT
Bench

- ○ Below Average
- ○ Average
- ○ Above Average
- ○ Whoa!

COMMENTS

APRIL 19)
THE SLOW YOUR ROLL

CALORIES

Giver 100.8

Receiver 96

EQUIPMENT

Rocking Chair

- ○ Below Average
- ○ Average
- ○ Above Average
- ○ Whoa!

COMMENTS

APRIL 20)

THE OPEN WIDE

CALORIES

Giver	35
Receiver	22

- ○ Below Average
- ○ Average
- ○ Above Average
- ○ Whoa!

COMMENTS

APRIL 21)
THE BACKUP

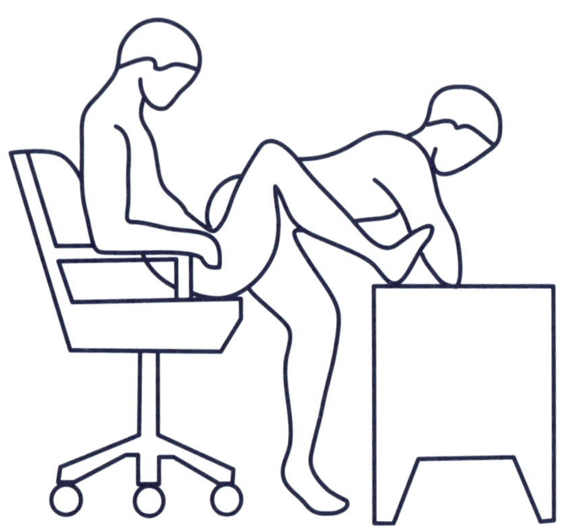

CALORIES

Giver 75.6

Receiver 54

EQUIPMENT

Chair

Desk

○ Below Average

○ Average

○ Above Average

○ Whoa!

COMMENTS

APRIL 22)
THE PIPE DREAM

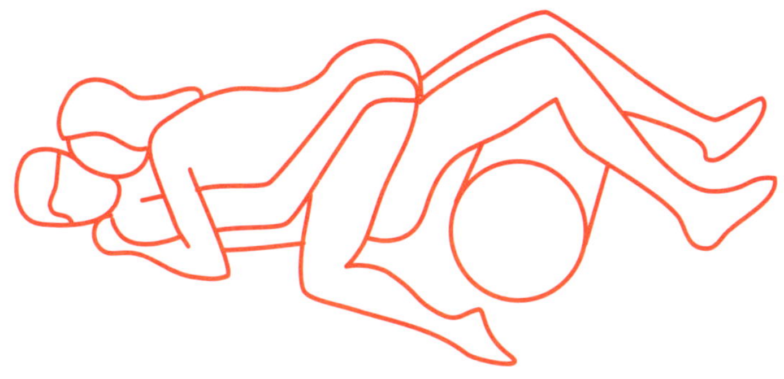

CALORIES

Giver 67.2

Receiver 48

EQUIPMENT

Large Pipe

- ○ Below Average
- ○ Average
- ○ Above Average
- ○ Whoa!

COMMENTS

APRIL 23)
THE FALLBACK

CALORIES

Giver	75.6
Receiver	54

EQUIPMENT

Chair

- ○ Below Average
- ○ Average
- ○ Above Average
- ○ Whoa!

COMMENTS

APRIL 24)
MANNEQUINS AFTER DARK

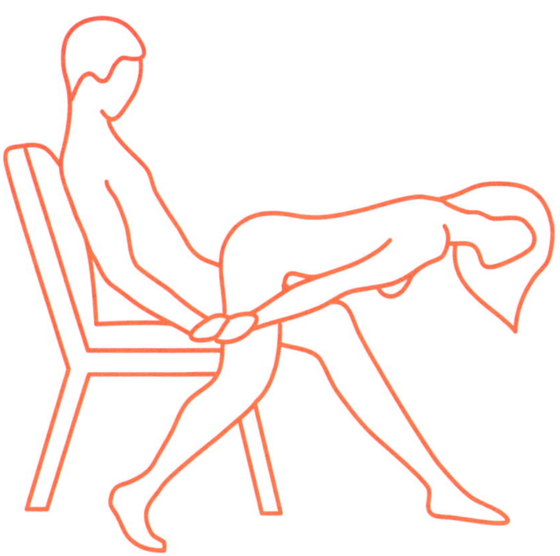

CALORIES		EQUIPMENT
Giver	75.6	Chair
Receiver	54	

- ○ Below Average
- ○ Average
- ○ Above Average
- ○ Whoa!

COMMENTS

APRIL 25)
ROUND THE BEND

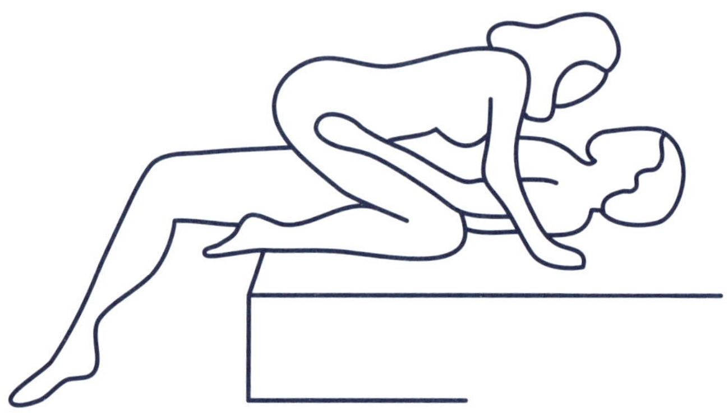

CALORIES

Giver 19

Receiver 54

EQUIPMENT

Bed

- ○ Below Average
- ○ Average
- ○ Above Average
- ○ Whoa!

COMMENTS

APRIL 26)

TANGLED UP IN YOU

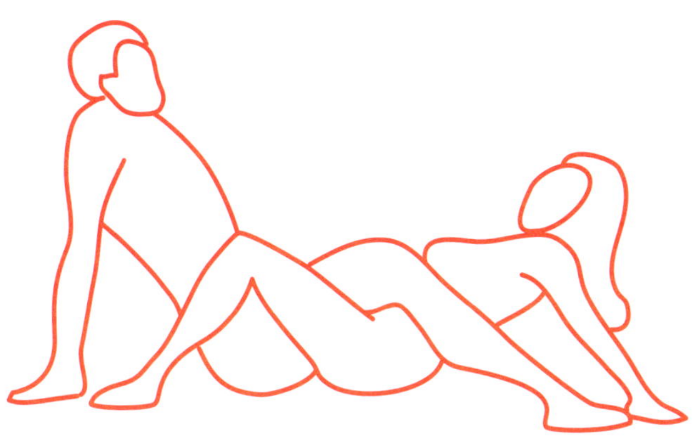

CALORIES

Giver 67.2

Receiver 48

- ○ Below Average
- ○ Average
- ○ Above Average
- ○ Whoa!

COMMENTS

APRIL 27)

ON THE TABLE

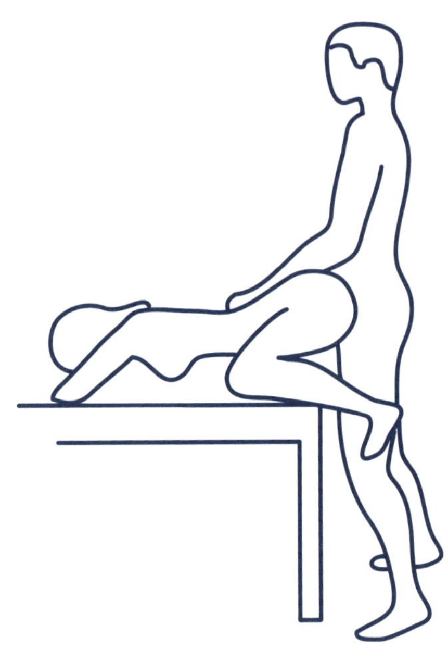

CALORIES

Giver 75.6

Receiver 54

EQUIPMENT

Table

- ○ Below Average
- ○ Average
- ○ Above Average
- ○ Whoa!

COMMENTS

APRIL 28)

THE ROCK ON

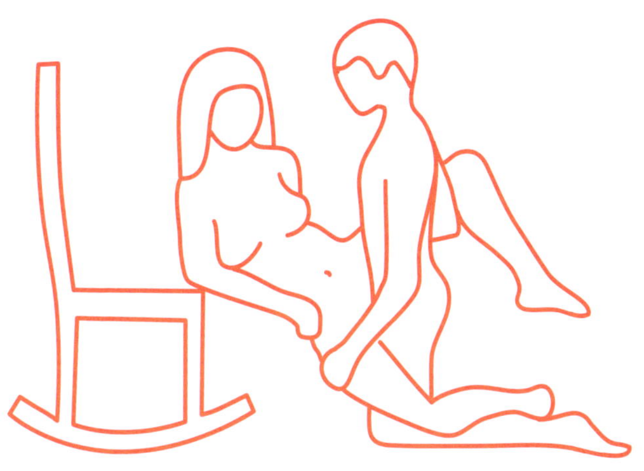

CALORIES

Giver 75.6

Receiver 48

EQUIPMENT

Rocking Chair

- ○ Below Average
- ○ Average
- ○ Above Average
- ○ Whoa!

COMMENTS

APRIL 29)
THE SIDESADDLE

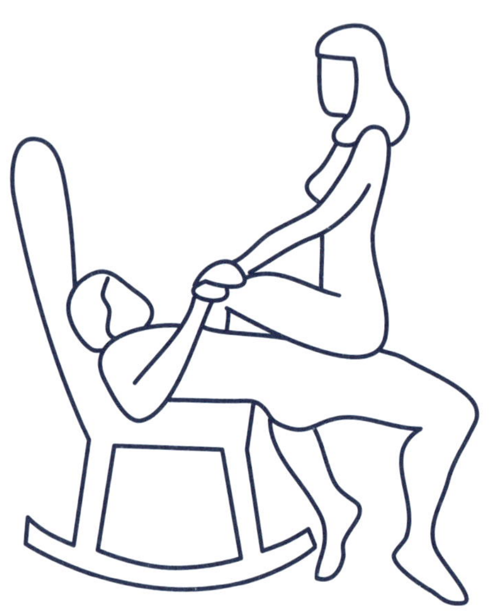

CALORIES

Giver 19

Receiver 66

EQUIPMENT

Rocking Chair

- ○ Below Average
- ○ Average
- ○ Above Average
- ○ Whoa!

COMMENTS

APRIL 30)
THE NO PAIN, NO GAIN

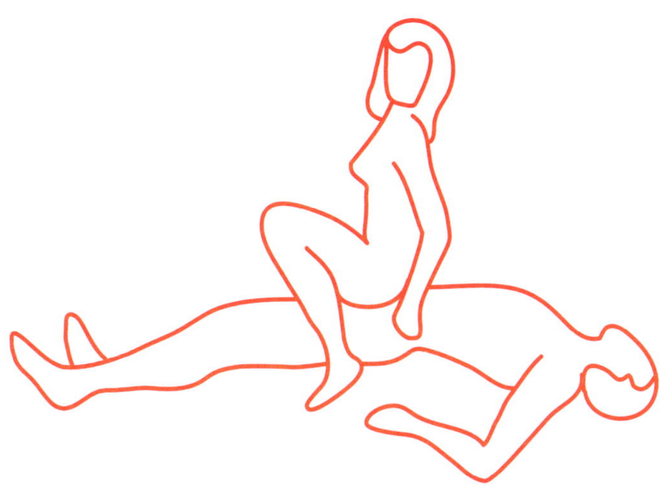

CALORIES

Giver 67.2

Receiver 54

EQUIPMENT

Aspirin

Ice Pack

- ○ Below Average
- ○ Average
- ○ Above Average
- ○ Whoa!

COMMENTS

MAY 01)

THE BACKSLASH

CALORIES

Giver 19

Receiver 54

EQUIPMENT

Table

- ○ Below Average
- ○ Average
- ○ Above Average
- ○ Whoa!

COMMENTS

MAY 02)
THE FRAME OF MIND

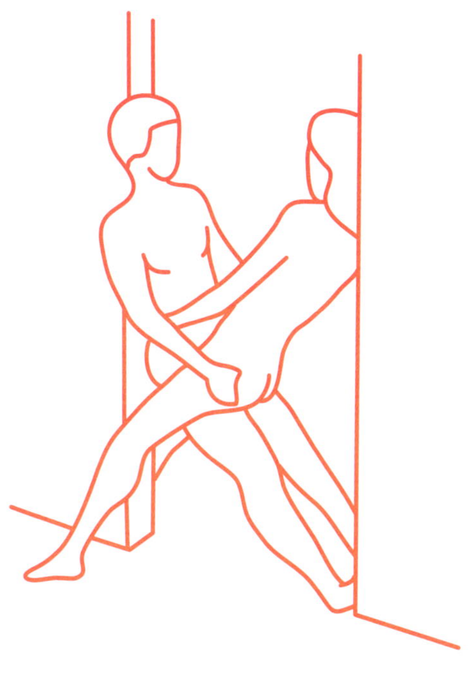

CALORIES

Giver 55

Receiver 40

EQUIPMENT

Doorframe

- ○ Below Average
- ○ Average
- ○ Above Average
- ○ Whoa!

COMMENTS

____

____

____

____

____

____

MAY 03)
THE SNORKELER

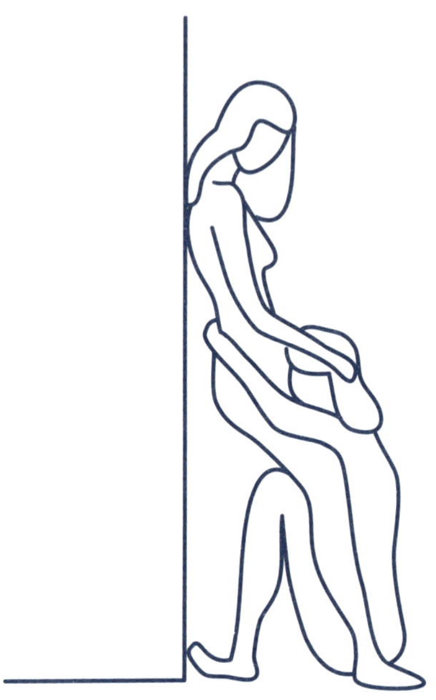

CALORIES

Giver 19

Receiver 13.6

EQUIPMENT

Wall

○ Below Average
○ Average
○ Above Average
○ Whoa!

COMMENTS

MAY 04)

SAVING GRACE

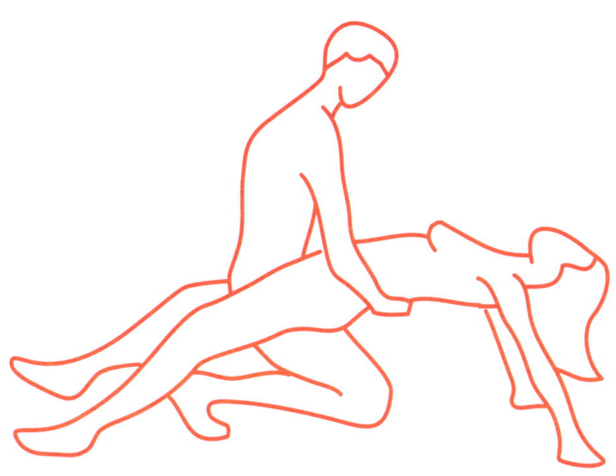

CALORIES

Giver 75.6

Receiver 84

- ○ Below Average
- ○ Average
- ○ Above Average
- ○ Whoa!

COMMENTS

____

____

____

____

____

____

MAY 05)
THE HOME FITNESS TEST

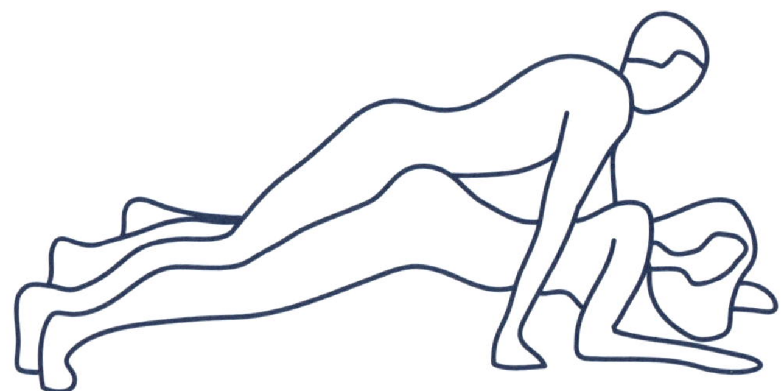

CALORIES
Giver 134.4
Receiver 96

EQUIPMENT
Exercise Checklist
Whistle

- ○ Below Average
- ○ Average
- ○ Above Average
- ○ Whoa!

COMMENTS

MAY 06)

THE PUFF PASTRY TWIST

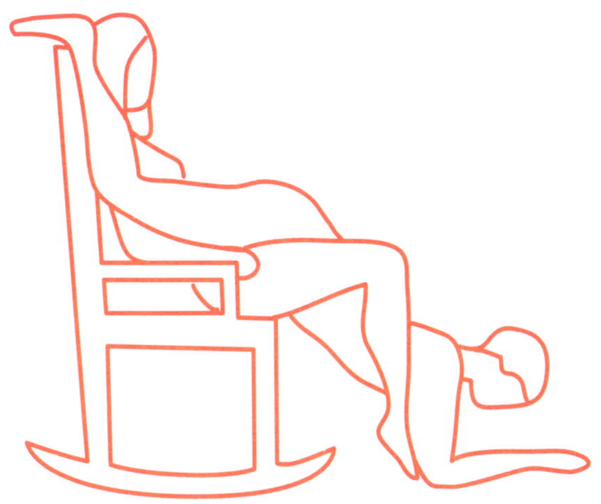

CALORIES

Giver 75.6

Receiver 48

EQUIPMENT

Rocking Chair

BENEFIT

Satisfies Sweet Tooth

○ Below Average

○ Average

○ Above Average

○ Whoa!

COMMENTS

____

____

____

____

____

____

MAY 07)
THE BENDS

CALORIES

Giver 13.6

Receiver 54

- ○ Below Average
- ○ Average
- ○ Above Average
- ○ Whoa!

COMMENTS

MAY 08)

THE LIFTOFF

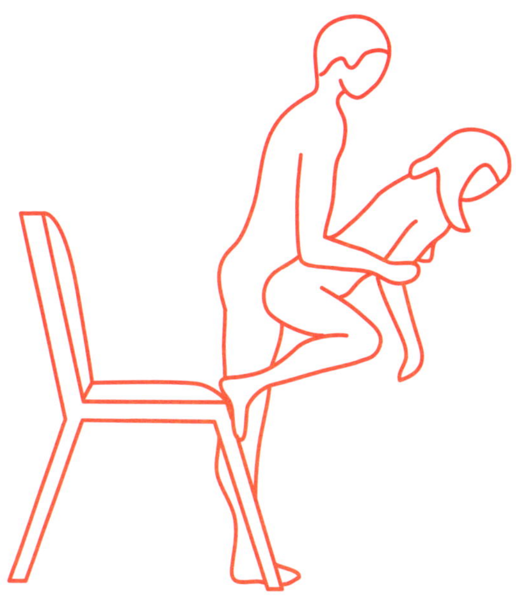

CALORIES

Giver 100.8

Receiver 120

EQUIPMENT

Chair

- ○ Below Average
- ○ Average
- ○ Above Average
- ○ Whoa!

COMMENTS

MAY 09)

THE LEAN BACK

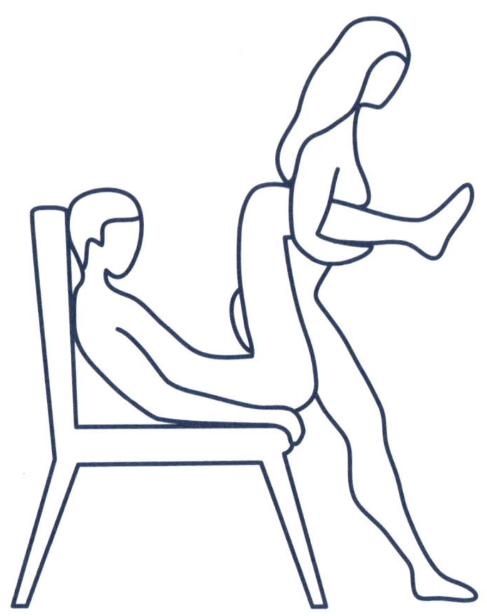

CALORIES

Giver 50

Receiver 72

EQUIPMENT

Chair

- ○ Below Average
- ○ Average
- ○ Above Average
- ○ Whoa!

COMMENTS

MAY 10)

THE LAZYBONE

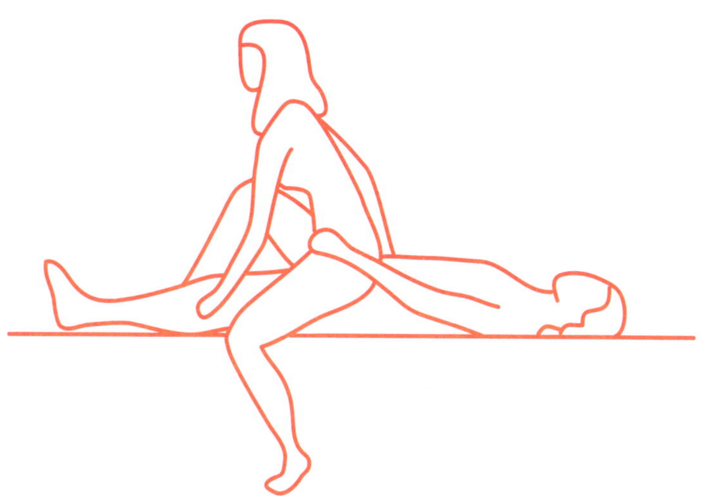

CALORIES

Giver 19

Receiver 48

BENEFIT

No Performance Anxiety

- ○ Below Average
- ○ Average
- ○ Above Average
- ○ Whoa!

COMMENTS

____

____

____

____

____

____

MAY 11)
THE MODIFIED PLANK

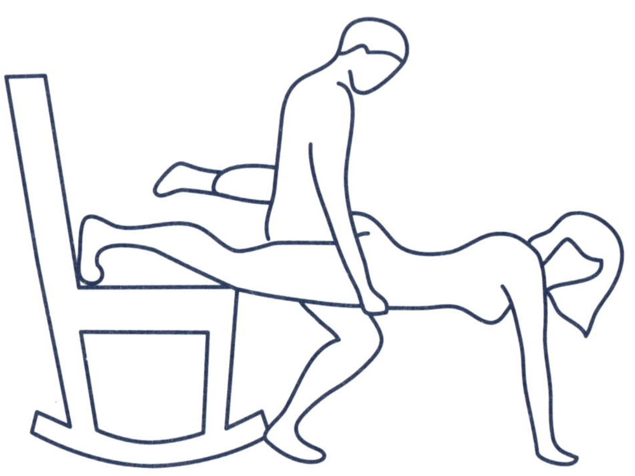

CALORIES
Giver 73
Receiver 96

EQUIPMENT
Rocking Chair

- ○ Below Average
- ○ Average
- ○ Above Average
- ○ Whoa!

COMMENTS

MAY 12)

THE GOOD CONVERSATIONALIST

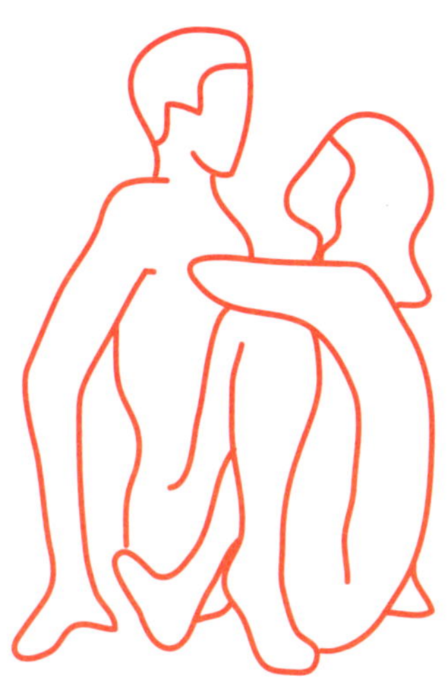

CALORIES		EQUIPMENT	BENEFIT
Giver	67.2	Thesaurus	Improved Vocabulary
Receiver	48		

- ○ Below Average
- ○ Average
- ○ Above Average
- ○ Whoa!

COMMENTS

MAY 13)
SHOULDERING THE BURDEN

CALORIES

Giver 75.6

Receiver 54

- ○ Below Average
- ○ Average
- ○ Above Average
- ○ Whoa!

COMMENTS

MAY 14)

THE DOWN DEEP

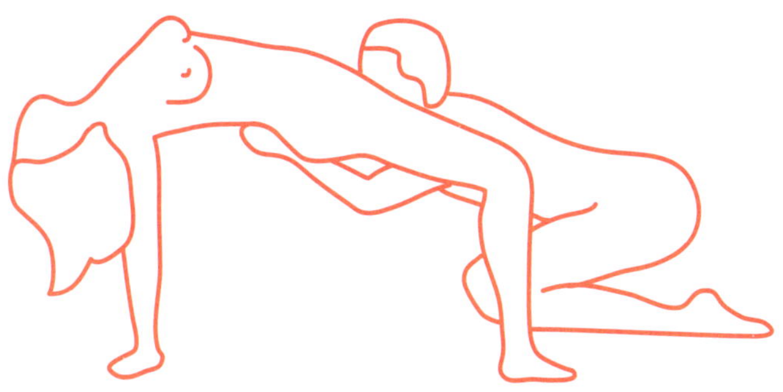

CALORIES

Giver 72

Receiver 88

- ○ Below Average
- ○ Average
- ○ Above Average
- ○ Whoa!

COMMENTS

MAY 15)
THE “HI THERE”

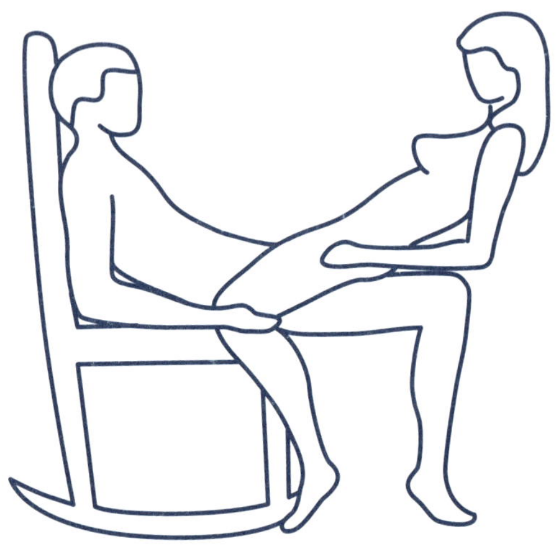

CALORIES

Giver 54

Receiver 38

EQUIPMENT

Rocking Chair

- ○ Below Average
- ○ Average
- ○ Above Average
- ○ Whoa!

COMMENTS

MAY 16)

FOLD IT IN

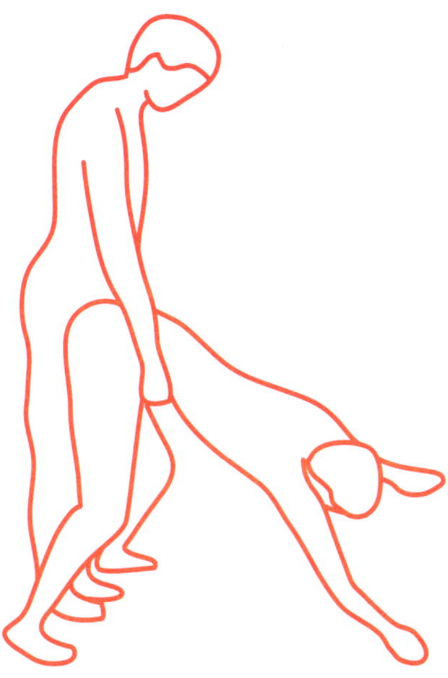

CALORIES

Giver	50.1
Receiver	75.6

- ○ Below Average
- ○ Average
- ○ Above Average
- ○ Whoa!

COMMENTS

MAY 17)

KING OF THE WORLD

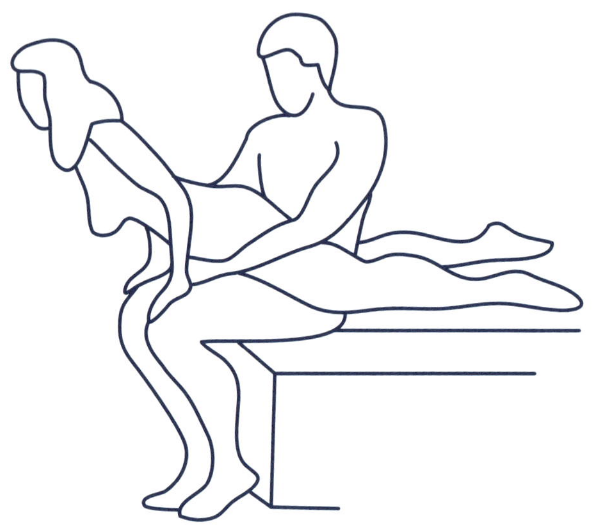

CALORIES

Giver 19

Receiver 48

EQUIPMENT

Bed

- ○ Below Average
- ○ Average
- ○ Above Average
- ○ Whoa!

COMMENTS

MAY 18)
THE ROLLER COASTER

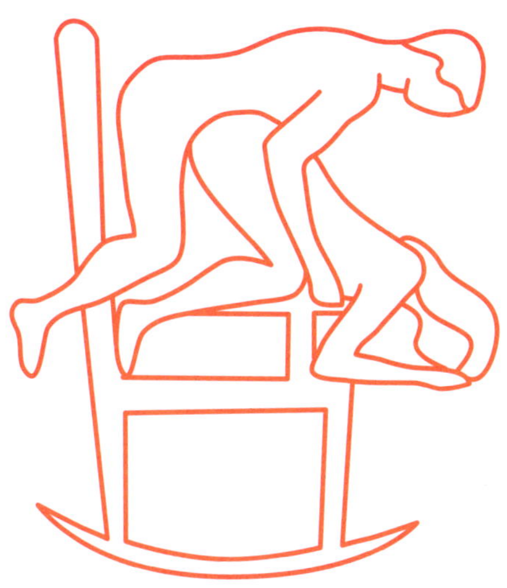

CALORIES		EQUIPMENT	HAZARD
Giver	49	Rocking Chair	Strained Calves
Receiver	54		

- ○ Below Average
- ○ Average
- ○ Above Average
- ○ Whoa!

COMMENTS

MAY 19)
THE BEST SEAT IN THE HOUSE

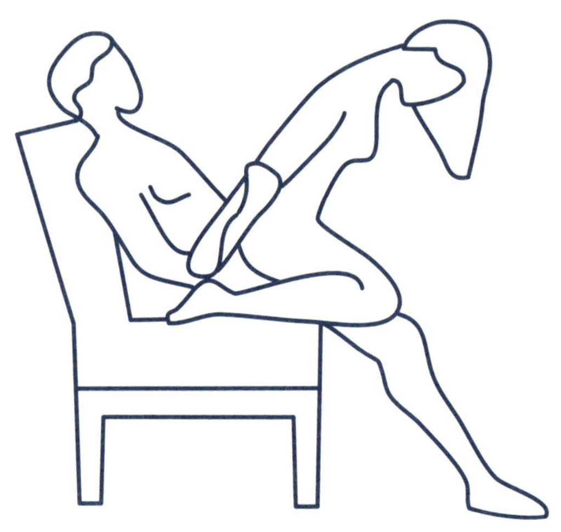

CALORIES

Giver 67.2

Receiver 96

EQUIPMENT

Chair

○ Below Average
○ Average
○ Above Average
○ Whoa!

COMMENTS

MAY 20)

THE FOR WHOM THE BELL TOLLS

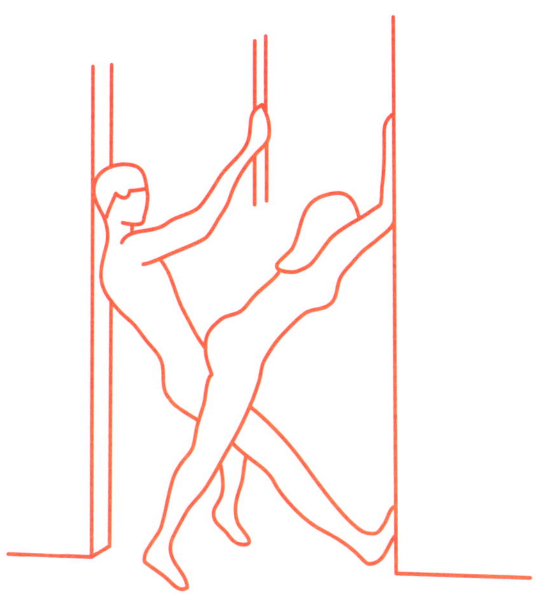

CALORIES

Giver 50.4

Receiver 48

EQUIPMENT

Rope, Doorframe, Earplugs, Bell

- ○ Below Average
- ○ Average
- ○ Above Average
- ○ Whoa!

COMMENTS

MAY 21)

THE SAFETY VEST

CALORIES

Giver 75.6

Receiver 54

- ○ Below Average
- ○ Average
- ○ Above Average
- ○ Whoa!

COMMENTS

MAY 22)

THE MATRIX

CALORIES		EQUIPMENT	BENEFIT
Giver	57	Rocking Chair	Guaranteed to Get a "Whoa"
Receiver	51		

- ○ Below Average
- ○ Average
- ○ Above Average
- ○ Whoa!

COMMENTS

MAY 23)

THE SPOON DRAWER

CALORIES

Giver 67.2

Receiver 48

- ○ Below Average
- ○ Average
- ○ Above Average
- ○ Whoa!

COMMENTS

MAY 24)
THE HELL-BENT

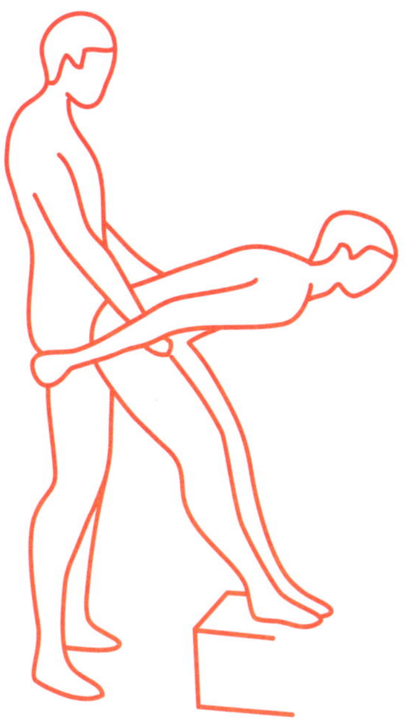

CALORIES

Giver	75.6
Receiver	54

EQUIPMENT

Stool

- ○ Below Average
- ○ Average
- ○ Above Average
- ○ Whoa!

COMMENTS

MAY 25)

SEX ON THE BRAIN

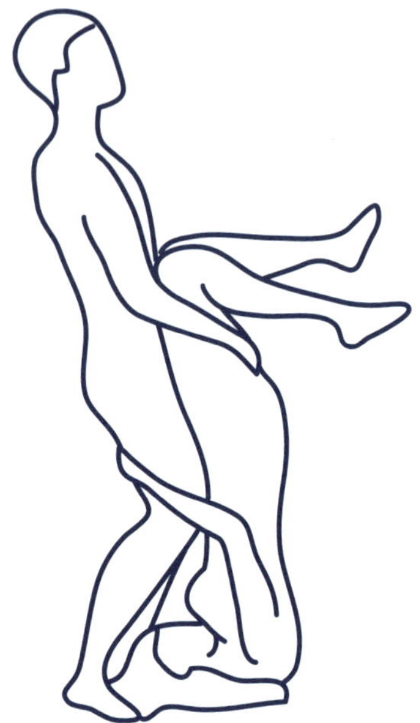

CALORIES

Giver	75.4
Receiver	82

HAZARD

Stiff Neck

- ○ Below Average
- ○ Average
- ○ Above Average
- ○ Whoa!

COMMENTS

MAY 26)
THE BENCH JOCKEY

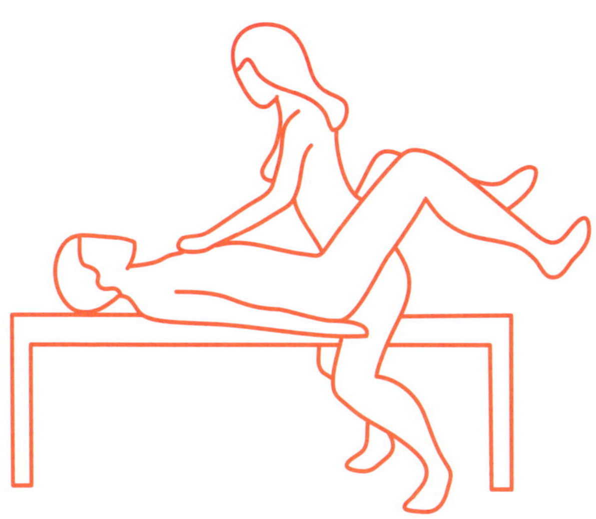

CALORIES

Giver 67.2

Receiver 66

EQUIPMENT

Bench

- ○ Below Average
- ○ Average
- ○ Above Average
- ○ Whoa!

COMMENTS

MAY 27)
THE RING-A-DING

CALORIES

Giver 167.2

Receiver 132

EQUIPMENT

Rings

○ Below Average
○ Average
○ Above Average
○ Whoa!

COMMENTS

MAY 28)
THE MEATBALL

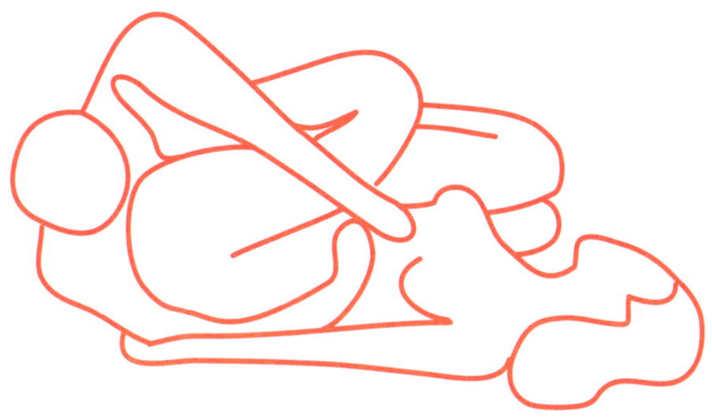

CALORIES

Giver 50.4

Receiver 48

HAZARD

Rolling off the Bed

- ○ Below Average
- ○ Average
- ○ Above Average
- ○ Whoa!

COMMENTS

MAY 29)
THE CATCH A VIBE

CALORIES

Giver 67.2

Receiver 84

- ○ Below Average
- ○ Average
- ○ Above Average
- ○ Whoa!

COMMENTS

MAY 30)
THE SPIDER

CALORIES

Giver 19

Receiver 54

EQUIPMENT

Swing

- ○ Below Average
- ○ Average
- ○ Above Average
- ○ Whoa!

COMMENTS

MAY 31)

THE HOT DESK

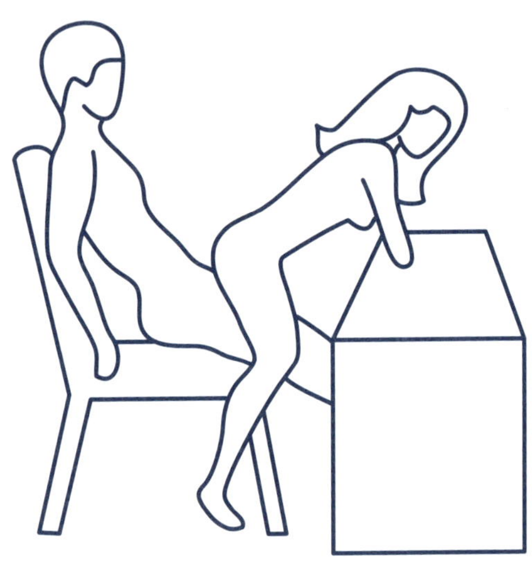

CALORIES

Giver	75.6
Receiver	54

EQUIPMENT

Chair

Desk

○ Below Average

○ Average

○ Above Average

○ Whoa!

COMMENTS

JUNE 01)

THE START YOUR ENGINES

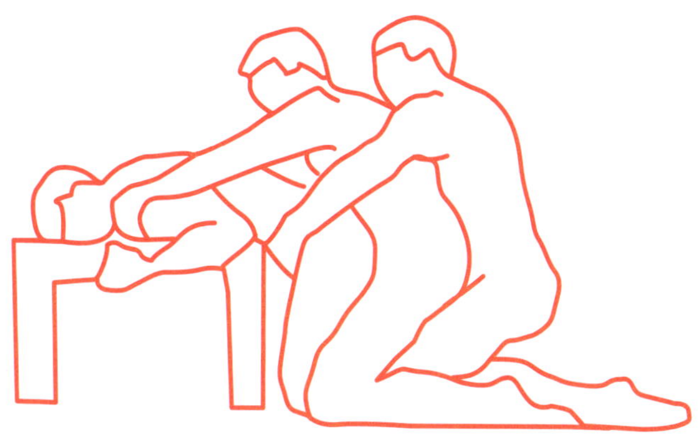

CALORIES

Giver	70.0
Giver and Receiver	94
Receiver	52

- ○ Below Average
- ○ Average
- ○ Above Average
- ○ Whoa!

COMMENTS

JUNE 02)
THE HOLD FAST

CALORIES
Giver 19
Receiver 48

EQUIPMENT
Mattress

HAZARD
Getting Stuck

- ○ Below Average
- ○ Average
- ○ Above Average
- ○ Whoa!

COMMENTS

JUNE 03)
THE WINDOW WASHER

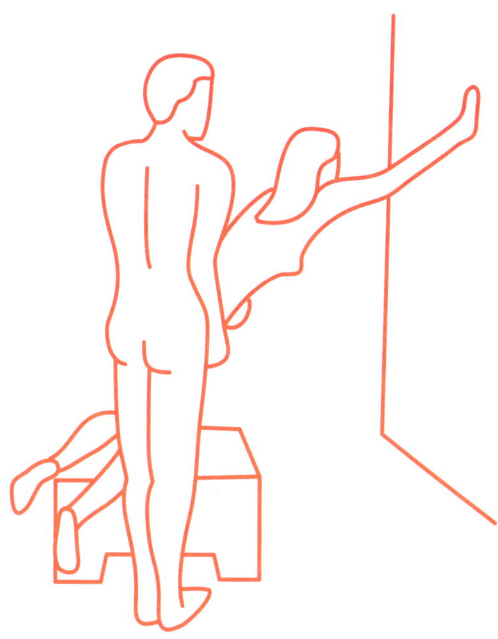

CALORIES

Giver 87.2
Receiver 96

EQUIPMENT

Stool
Wall

- ○ Below Average
- ○ Average
- ○ Above Average
- ○ Whoa!

COMMENTS

____

____

____

____

____

____

JUNE 04)

THE DOG AND PONY SHOW

CALORIES

Giver 92.4

Receiver 84

- ○ Below Average
- ○ Average
- ○ Above Average
- ○ Whoa!

COMMENTS

JUNE 05)

THE WRECKING BALL

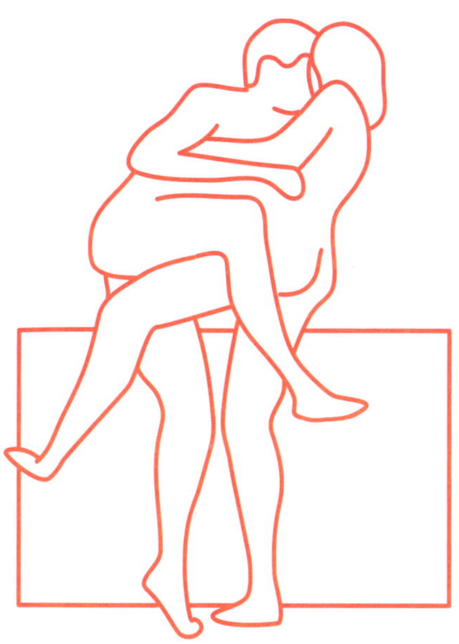

CALORIES

Giver	67.8
Receiver	48

EQUIPMENT

Wall

- ○ Below Average
- ○ Average
- ○ Above Average
- ○ Whoa!

COMMENTS

JUNE 06)

A WALK TO REMEMBER

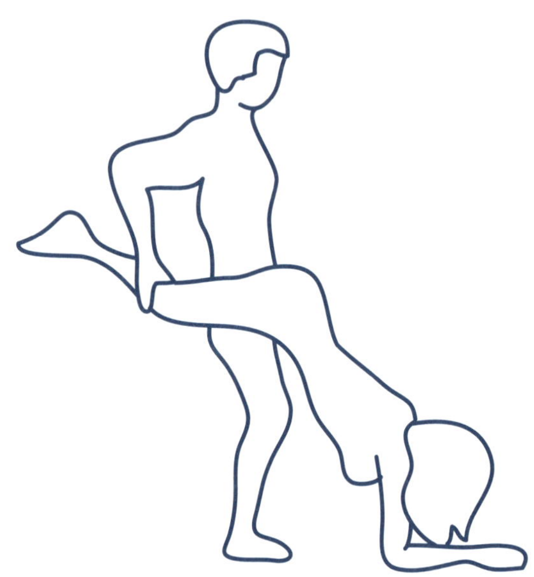

CALORIES

Giver 100.8

Receiver 96

- ○ Below Average
- ○ Average
- ○ Above Average
- ○ Whoa!

COMMENTS

JUNE 07)
THE BOW AND ARROW

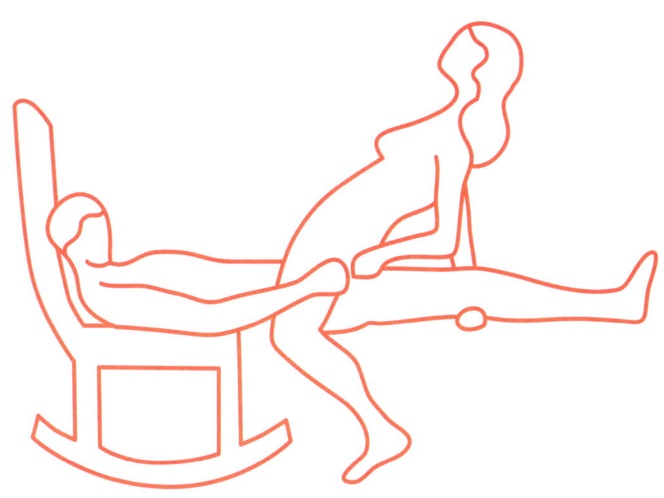

CALORIES
Giver 67.2
Receiver 96

EQUIPMENT
Rocking Chair

- ○ Below Average
- ○ Average
- ○ Above Average
- ○ Whoa!

COMMENTS

JUNE 08)

THE HANG BANG

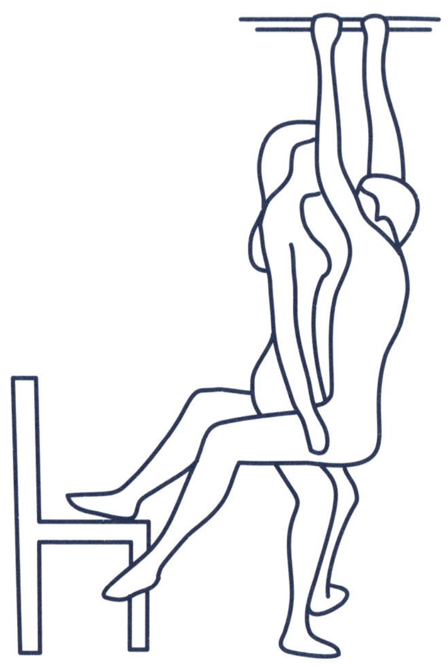

CALORIES

Giver 112

Receiver 96

EQUIPMENT

Chair

Pull-Up Bar

- ○ Below Average
- ○ Average
- ○ Above Average
- ○ Whoa!

COMMENTS

JUNE 09)
THE PINBALL WIZARD

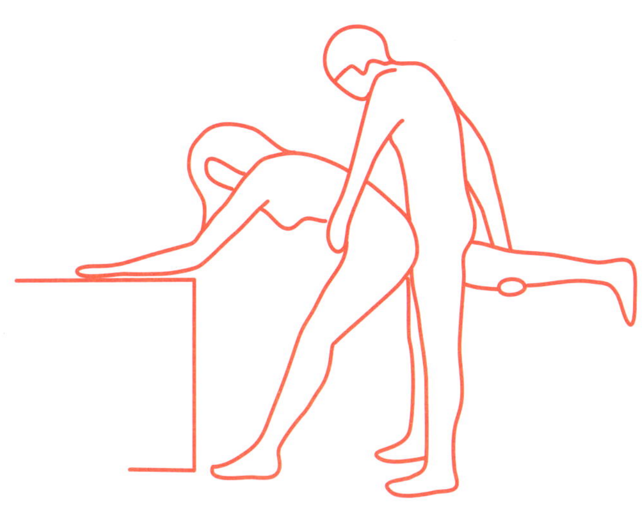

CALORIES		EQUIPMENT	HAZARD
Giver	67.2	Bed	Do Not Tilt
Receiver	48		

- ○ Below Average
- ○ Average
- ○ Above Average
- ○ Whoa!

COMMENTS

JUNE 10)

THE REARRANGEMENT

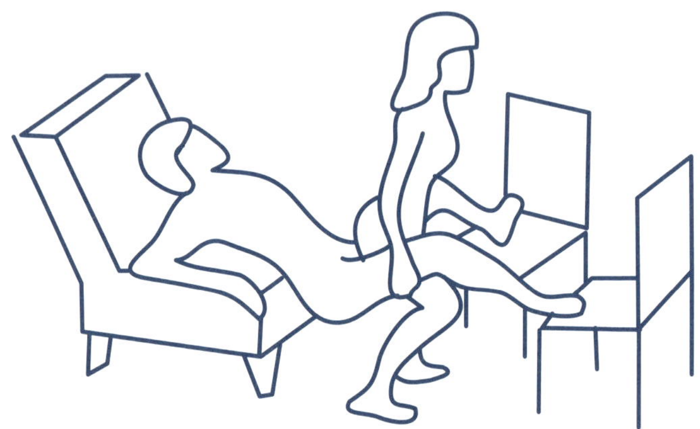

CALORIES		EQUIPMENT	BENEFIT
Giver	67.2	Three Chairs	New Perspective
Receiver	66		

- ○ Below Average
- ○ Average
- ○ Above Average
- ○ Whoa!

COMMENTS

JUNE 11)

THE SEXYBACK

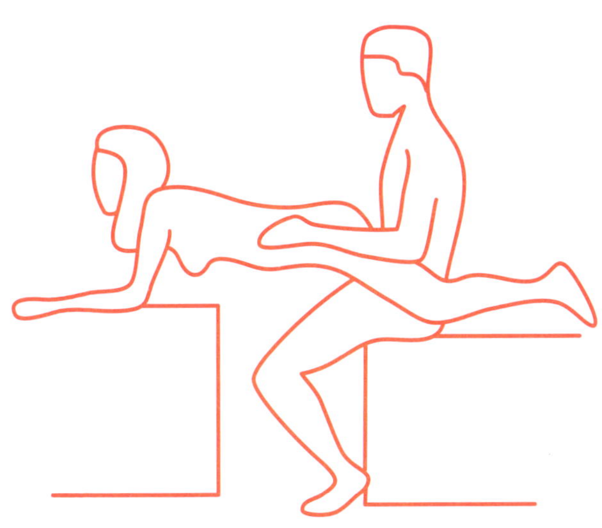

CALORIES	
Giver	19
Receiver	48

EQUIPMENT

Two Beds

- ○ Below Average
- ○ Average
- ○ Above Average
- ○ Whoa!

COMMENTS

JUNE 12)

FACE VALUE

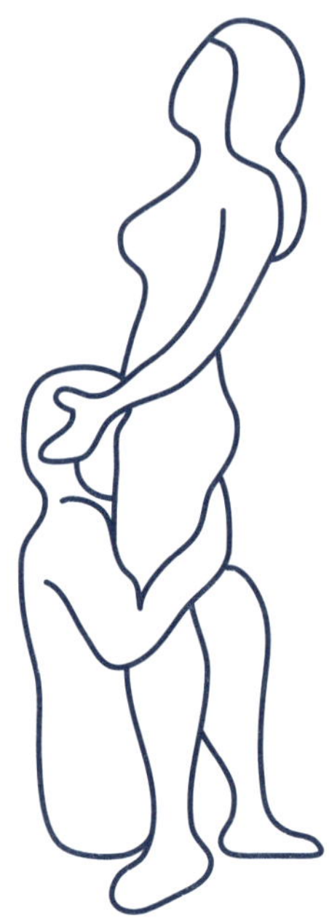

CALORIES

Giver 19

Receiver 48

- ○ Below Average
- ○ Average
- ○ Above Average
- ○ Whoa!

COMMENTS

____

____

____

____

____

____

JUNE 13)

THE BONGO PLAYER

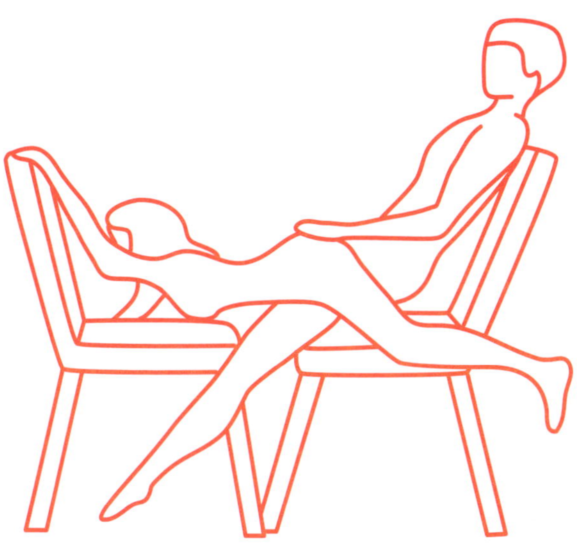

CALORIES		EQUIPMENT	BENEFIT	
Giver	19	Two Chairs	Saves Time on Drumming Practice	○ Below Average
Receiver	54			○ Average
				○ Above Average
				○ Whoa!

COMMENTS

JUNE 14)
THE DEEP BENCH

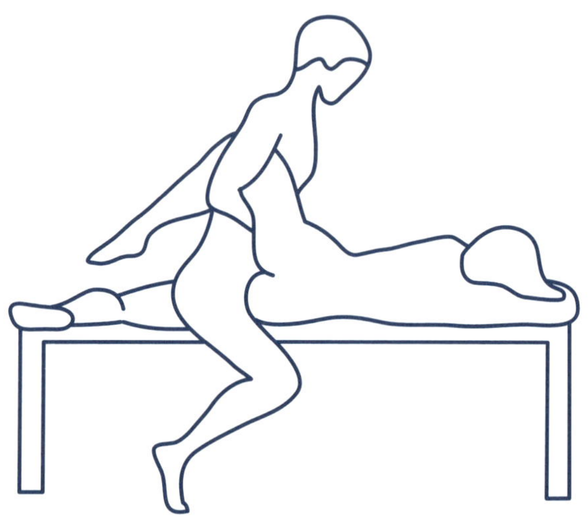

CALORIES

Giver 75.6

Receiver 48

EQUIPMENT

Bench

○ Below Average

○ Average

○ Above Average

○ Whoa!

COMMENTS

JUNE 15)

THE RIGHT ANGLE STUFF

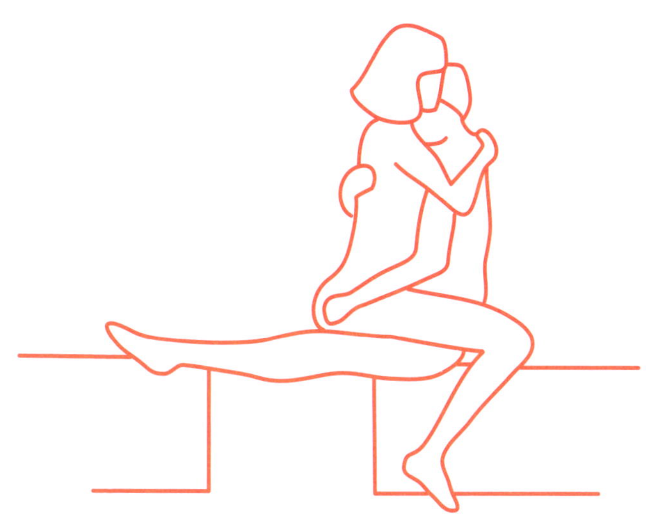

CALORIES

Giver 67.2

Receiver 66

EQUIPMENT

Two Beds

- ○ Below Average
- ○ Average
- ○ Above Average
- ○ Whoa!

COMMENTS

___

___

___

___

___

___

JUNE 16)
THE STANDING ROOM ONLY

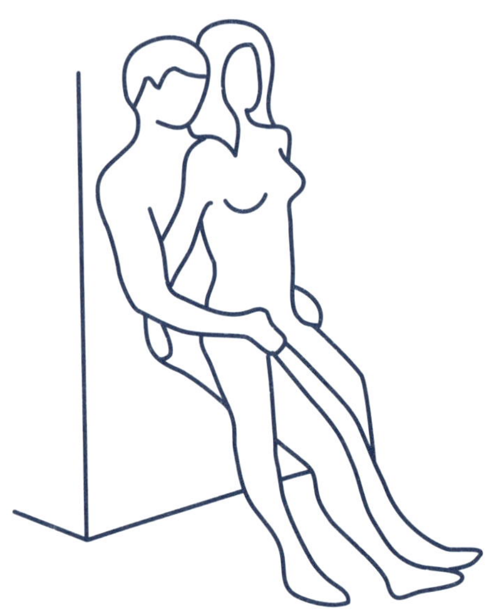

CALORIES

Giver 75.6

Receiver 66

EQUIPMENT

Wall

- ○ Below Average
- ○ Average
- ○ Above Average
- ○ Whoa!

COMMENTS

JUNE 17)

THE HORNY TOAD

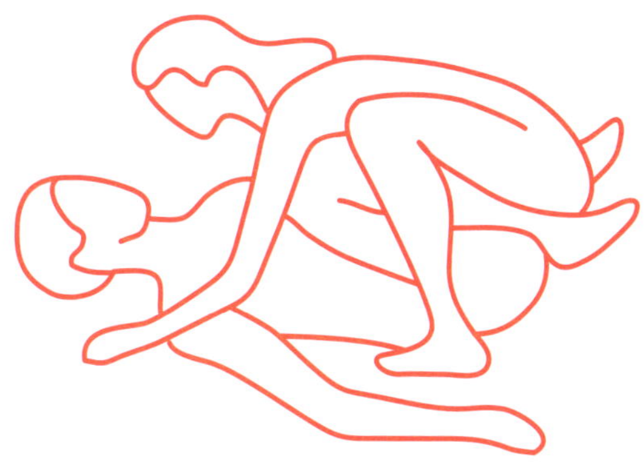

CALORIES

Giver 55

Receiver 72

○ Below Average

○ Average

○ Above Average

○ Whoa!

COMMENTS

JUNE 18)
THE MACRAME STITCH

CALORIES

Giver 75.6

Receiver 54

EQUIPMENT

Rocking Chair

- ○ Below Average
- ○ Average
- ○ Above Average
- ○ Whoa!

COMMENTS

JUNE 19)
THE CAN-CAN

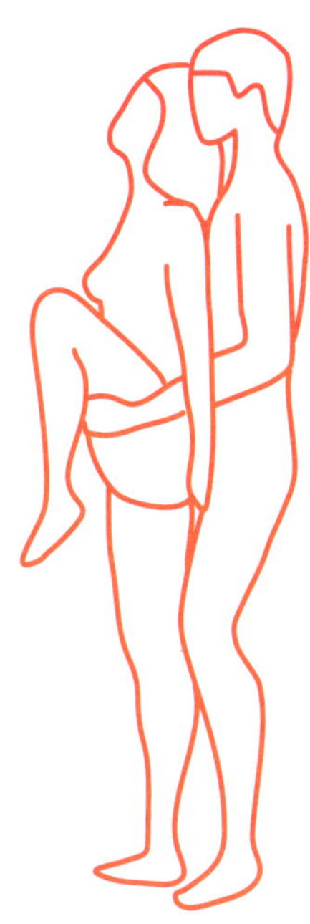

CALORIES
Giver 67.2
Receiver 48

EQUIPMENT
Tights
High Heels
Show Tunes

- ○ Below Average
- ○ Average
- ○ Above Average
- ○ Whoa!

COMMENTS

JUNE 20)

THE HORIZONTAL PASO DOBLE

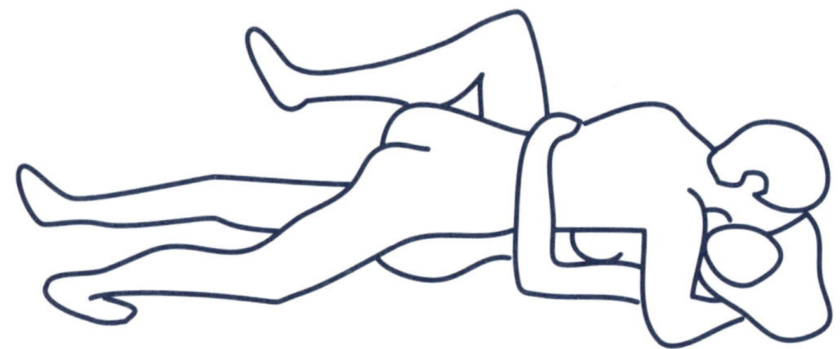

CALORIES

Giver 75.6

Receiver 66

- ○ Below Average
- ○ Average
- ○ Above Average
- ○ Whoa!

COMMENTS

JUNE 21)

THE BACKSEAT DRIVER

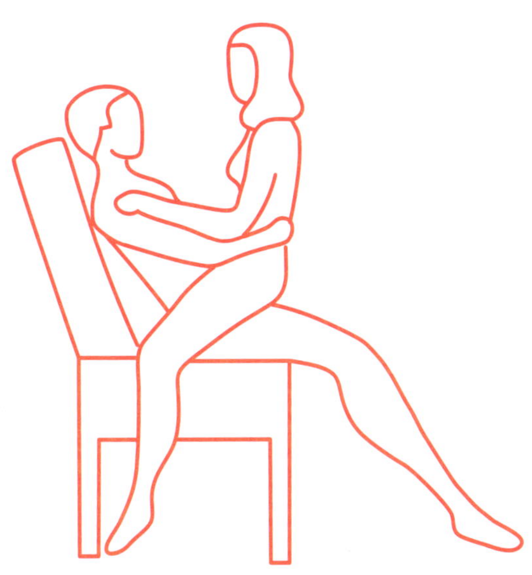

CALORIES

Giver 10

Receiver 54

EQUIPMENT

Chair

- ○ Below Average
- ○ Average
- ○ Above Average
- ○ Whoa!

COMMENTS

JUNE 22)

PUTTING THE "US" IN RHOMBUS

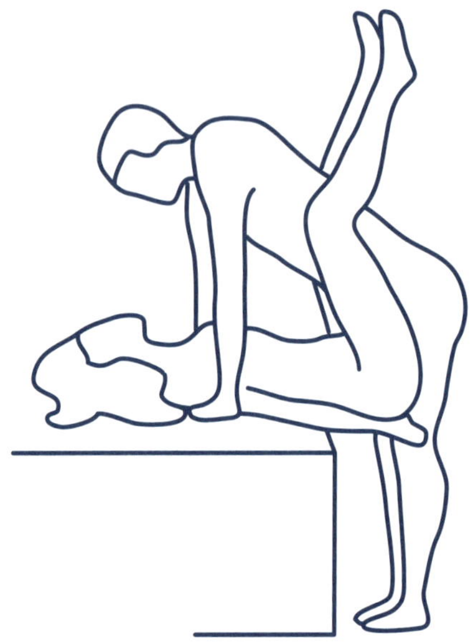

CALORIES

Giver 75.6

Receiver 54

EQUIPMENT

Bed

- ○ Below Average
- ○ Average
- ○ Above Average
- ○ Whoa!

COMMENTS

JUNE 23)

THE FRONT LOAD

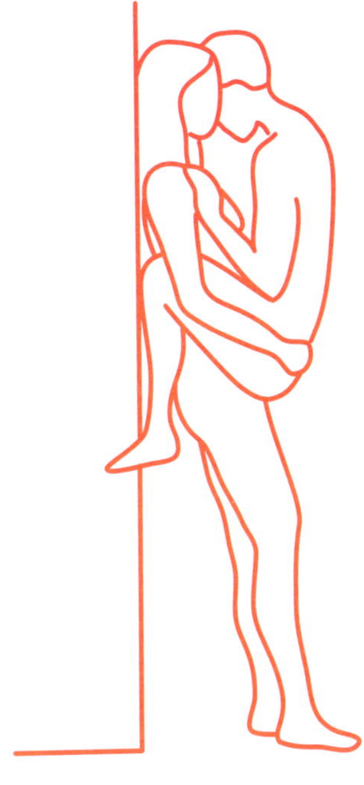

CALORIES

Giver 19

Receiver 72

EQUIPMENT

Wall

○ Below Average

○ Average

○ Above Average

○ Whoa!

COMMENTS

JUNE 24)
THE SEXY PRETZEL

CALORIES

Giver 75.6

Receiver 54

- ○ Below Average
- ○ Average
- ○ Above Average
- ○ Whoa!

COMMENTS

JUNE 25)

THE KNEE-JERK REACTION

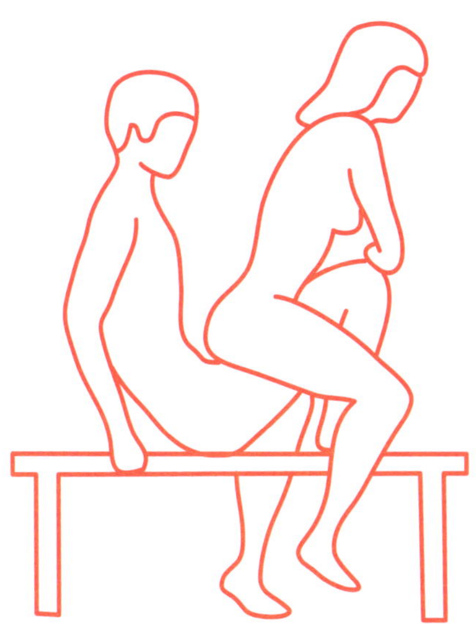

CALORIES		EQUIPMENT
Giver	70.0	Bench
Receiver	54	

- ○ Below Average
- ○ Average
- ○ Above Average
- ○ Whoa!

COMMENTS

JUNE 26)

THE FIRE POLE

CALORIES

Giver 75.6

Receiver 54

EQUIPMENT

Pole

- ○ Below Average
- ○ Average
- ○ Above Average
- ○ Whoa!

COMMENTS

JUNE 27)

THE "HONEY, I'M HOME"

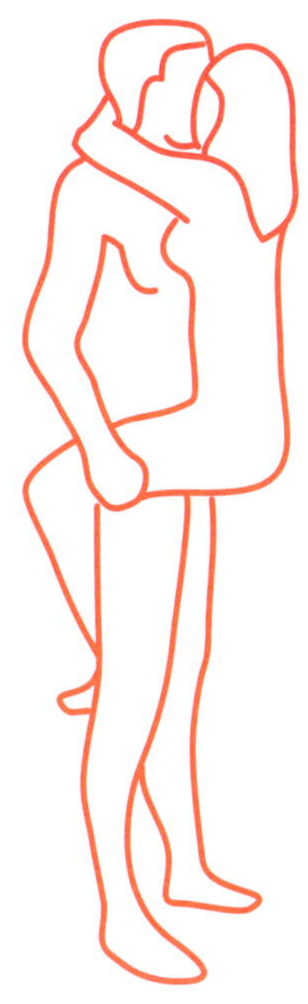

CALORIES

Giver	100.8
Receiver	66

- ○ Below Average
- ○ Average
- ○ Above Average
- ○ Whoa!

COMMENTS

JUNE 28)
THE BREAK A LEG

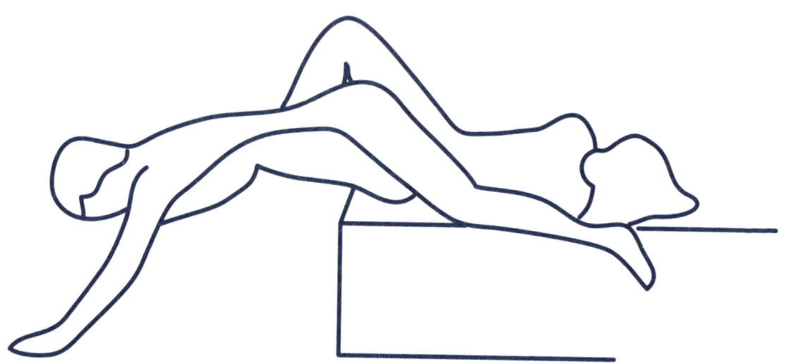

CALORIES

Giver 75.4

Receiver 54

EQUIPMENT

Mattress

- ○ Below Average
- ○ Average
- ○ Above Average
- ○ Whoa!

COMMENTS

JUNE 29)

THE SLINGSHOT

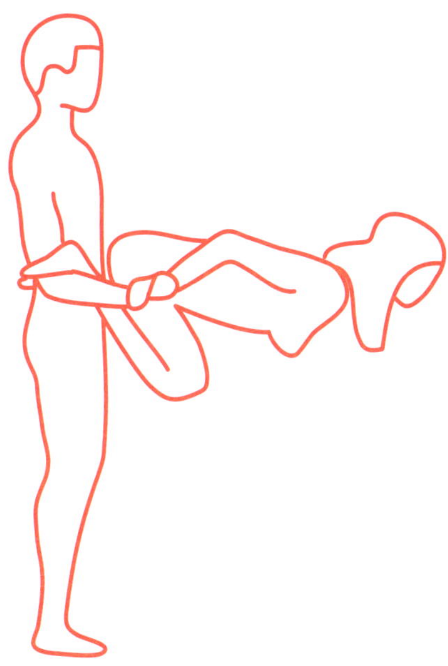

CALORIES

Giver 100.8

Receiver 132

- ○ Below Average
- ○ Average
- ○ Above Average
- ○ Whoa!

COMMENTS

___

___

___

___

___

___

JUNE 30)
THE STARTING GATE

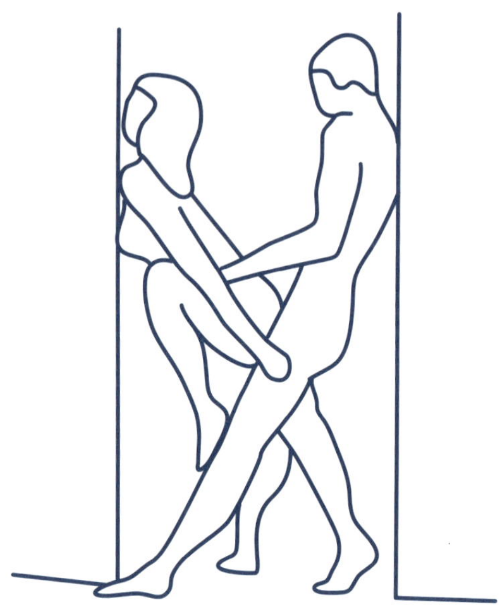

CALORIES

Giver 75.6

Receiver 66

EQUIPMENT

Doorframe

○ Below Average
○ Average
○ Above Average
○ Whoa!

COMMENTS

JULY 01)

THE FIND A PENNY

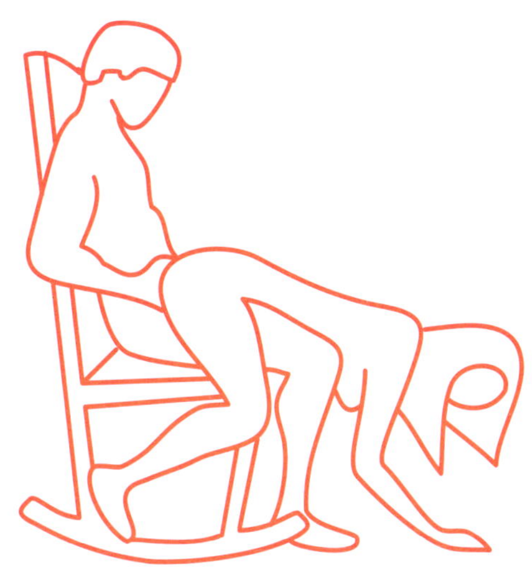

CALORIES		EQUIPMENT	
Giver	19	Rocking Chair	○ Below Average
Receiver	60		○ Average
			○ Above Average
			○ Whoa!

COMMENTS

JULY 02)

CREW PRACTICE

CALORIES

Giver	67.2
Receiver	54

EQUIPMENT

Chair

- ○ Below Average
- ○ Average
- ○ Above Average
- ○ Whoa!

COMMENTS

JULY 03)
SEX IN ITALICS

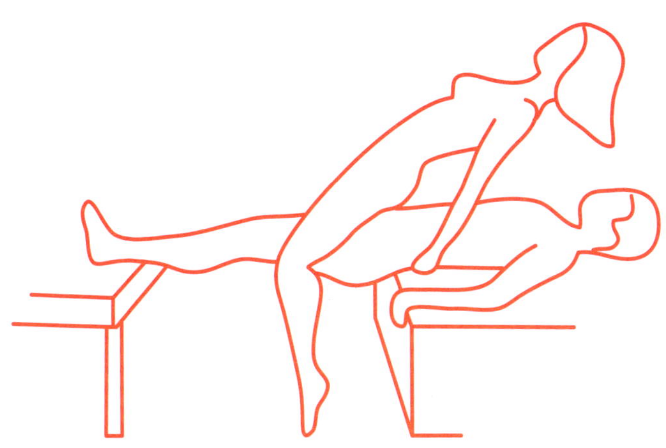

CALORIES		EQUIPMENT
Giver	67.2	Bed
Receiver	96	Desk

- ○ Below Average
- ○ Average
- ○ Above Average
- ○ Whoa!

COMMENTS

JULY 04)

THE FOURTH OF JULY HOT DOG

CALORIES

Giver 75.6

Receiver 66

- ○ Below Average
- ○ Average
- ○ Above Average
- ○ Whoa!

COMMENTS

JULY 05)

THE JOAN OF ARCH

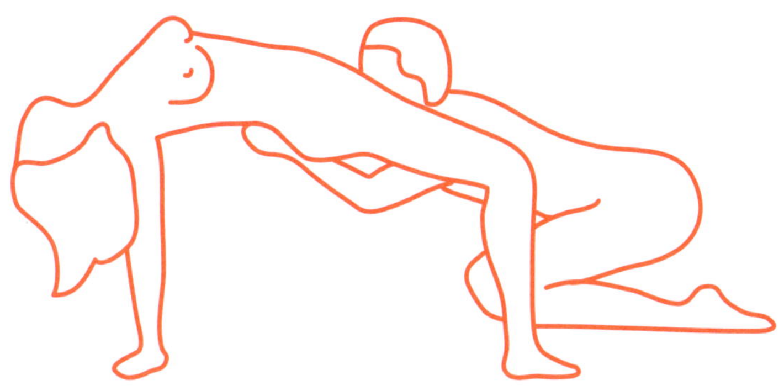

CALORIES

Giver	72
Receiver	88

- ○ Below Average
- ○ Average
- ○ Above Average
- ○ Whoa!

COMMENTS

JULY 06)
THE LUMBERJACKS

CALORIES

Giver	117.6
Receiver	84

EQUIPMENT

Rocking Chair

- ○ Below Average
- ○ Average
- ○ Above Average
- ○ Whoa!

COMMENTS

JULY 07)

THE MUNCHIES

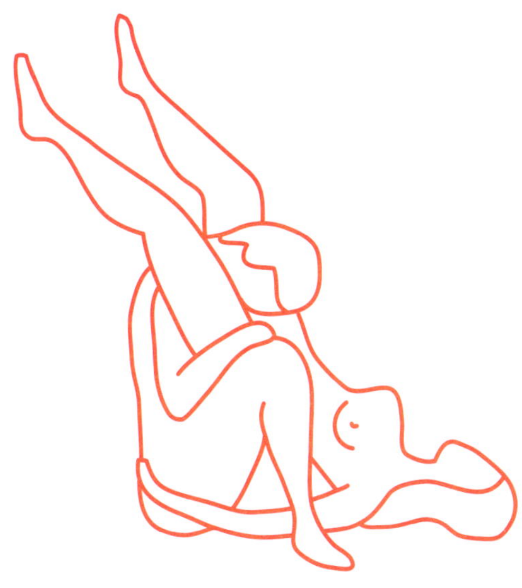

CALORIES

Giver	67.2
Receiver	96

- ○ Below Average
- ○ Average
- ○ Above Average
- ○ Whoa!

COMMENTS

JULY 08)

THE U-TURN

CALORIES

Giver 75.4

Receiver 66

EQUIPMENT

Rocking Chair

○ Below Average

○ Average

○ Above Average

○ Whoa!

COMMENTS

JULY 09)

THE MUD FLAPPER

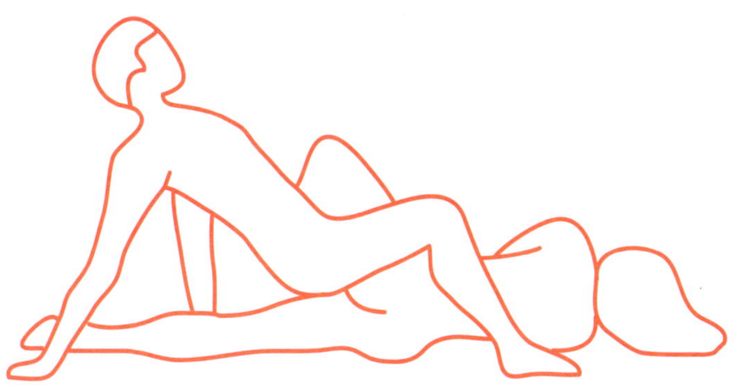

CALORIES

Giver	75.6
Receiver	51

- ○ Below Average
- ○ Average
- ○ Above Average
- ○ Whoa!

COMMENTS

JULY 10)
THE PRESSED SHIRT

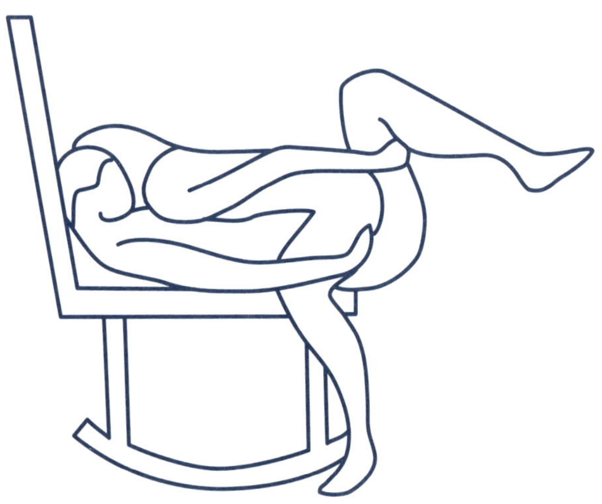

CALORIES		EQUIPMENT	BENEFIT
Giver	67.2	Steaming, Hot Bodies	No Need for Ironing
Receiver	54		

- ○ Below Average
- ○ Average
- ○ Above Average
- ○ Whoa!

COMMENTS

JULY 11)
THE SURF'S UP

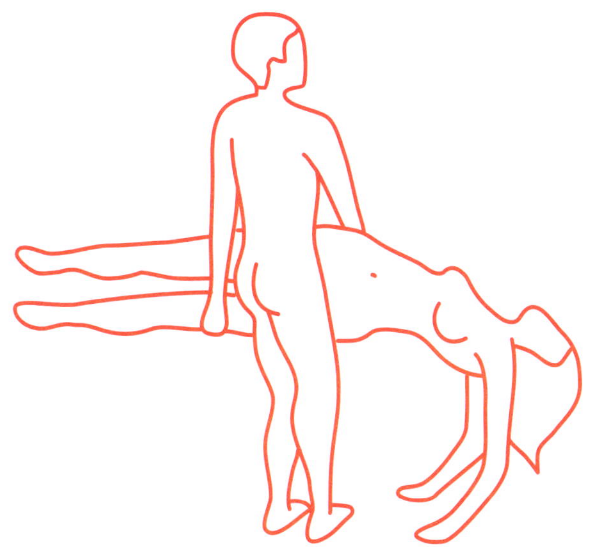

CALORIES
Giver 100.6
Receiver 96

EQUIPMENT
Optional:
Wet Suit

- ○ Below Average
- ○ Average
- ○ Above Average
- ○ Whoa!

COMMENTS

JULY 12)
THE GIRLS JUST WANT TO HAVE FUN

CALORIES
Giver 61
Receiver 61

EQUIPMENT
Two Chairs

- ○ Below Average
- ○ Average
- ○ Above Average
- ○ Whoa!

COMMENTS

JULY 13)
THE SIDEWINDER

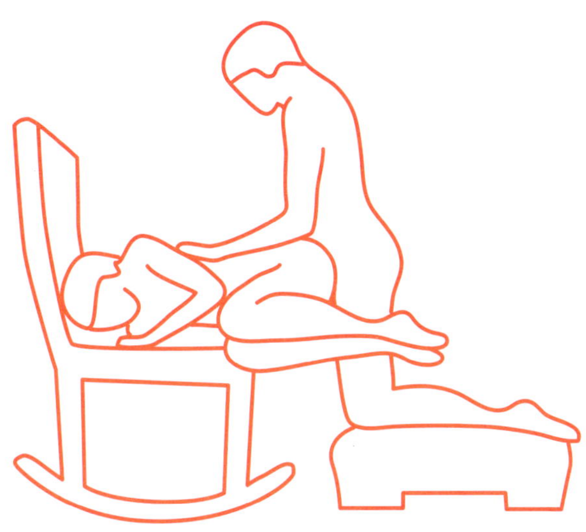

CALORIES		EQUIPMENT
Giver	75.6	Rocking Chair
Receiver	48	Stool

- ○ Below Average
- ○ Average
- ○ Above Average
- ○ Whoa!

COMMENTS

JULY 14)
THE ARMCHAIR TRAVELER

CALORIES		EQUIPMENT	HAZARD
Giver	50.4	Rocking Chair	Getting Stuck
Receiver	54		

- ○ Below Average
- ○ Average
- ○ Above Average
- ○ Whoa!

COMMENTS

JULY 15)

THE R-RATED R & R

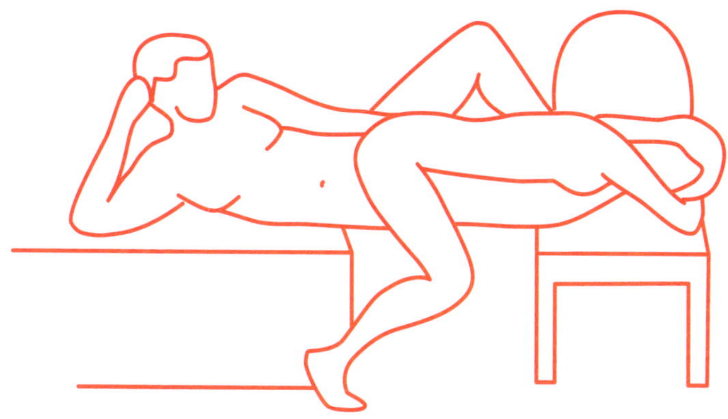

CALORIES		EQUIPMENT
Giver	19	Chair
Receiver	66	Bed

- ○ Below Average
- ○ Average
- ○ Above Average
- ○ Whoa!

COMMENTS

JULY 16)
BUILDING BRIDGES

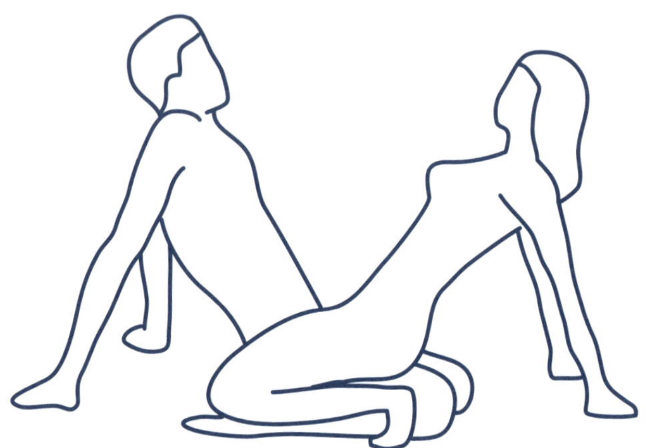

CALORIES

Giver 67.2

Receiver 48

- ○ Below Average
- ○ Average
- ○ Above Average
- ○ Whoa!

COMMENTS

JULY 17)
THE STAND AND DELIVER

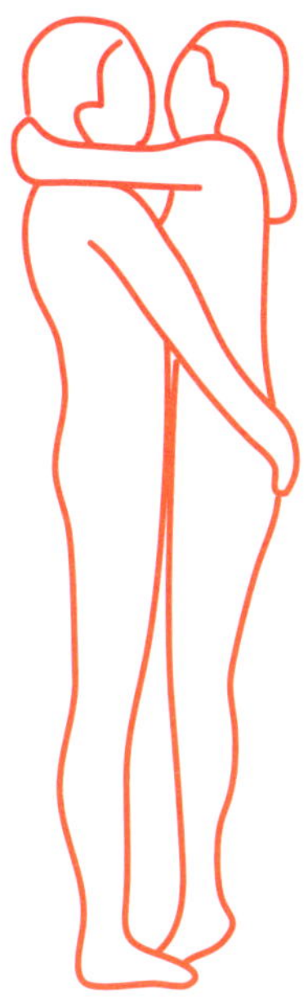

CALORIES

Giver 19

Receiver 36

○ Below Average

○ Average

○ Above Average

○ Whoa!

COMMENTS

JULY 18)

THE OLD AND THE RESTLESS

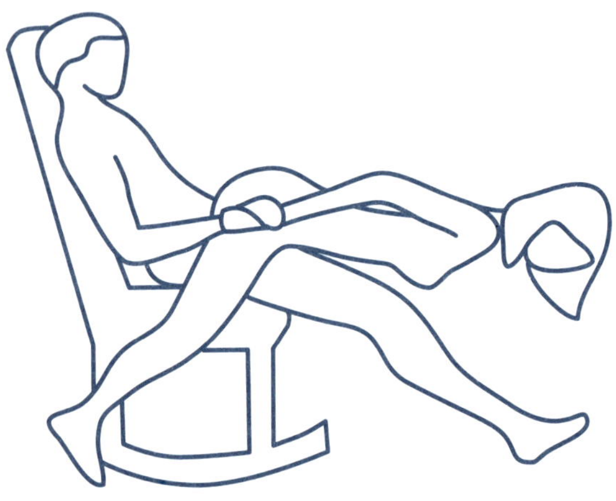

CALORIES
Giver 19
Receiver 48

EQUIPMENT
Rocking Chair

HAZARD
Motion Sickness

○ Below Average
○ Average
○ Above Average
○ Whoa!

COMMENTS

JULY 19)

THE BEST IN SHOW

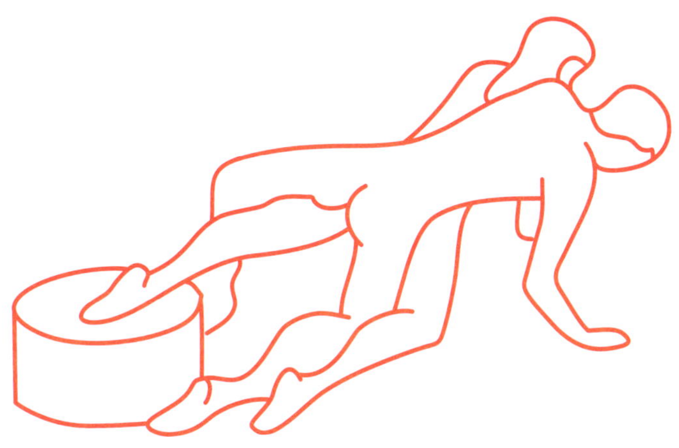

CALORIES		EQUIPMENT
Giver	92.9	Stool
Receiver	66	

- ○ Below Average
- ○ Average
- ○ Above Average
- ○ Whoa!

COMMENTS

JULY 20)
THE SIDESWIPE

CALORIES

Giver 54

Receiver 63

○ Below Average

○ Average

○ Above Average

○ Whoa!

COMMENTS

JULY 21)

COMING TO A HEAD

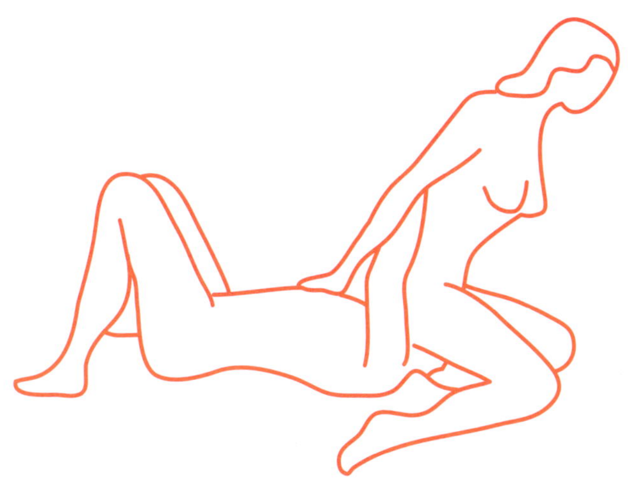

CALORIES

Giver 19

Receiver 54

- ○ Below Average
- ○ Average
- ○ Above Average
- ○ Whoa!

COMMENTS

JULY 22)

NAP TIME

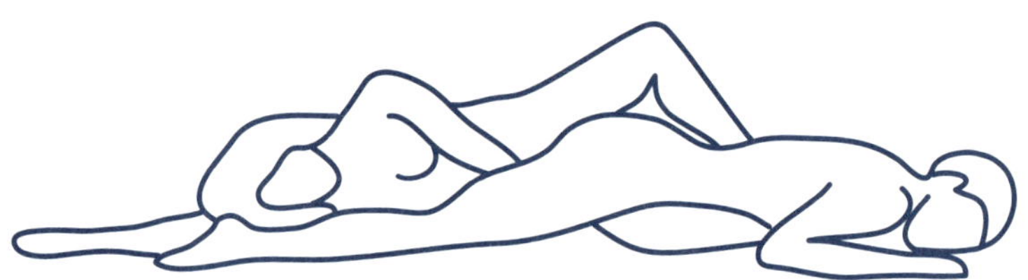

CALORIES

Giver 19

Receiver 13.6

EQUIPMENT

Pillow

- ○ Below Average
- ○ Average
- ○ Above Average
- ○ Whoa!

COMMENTS

JULY 23)
PUT IT IN THE CART

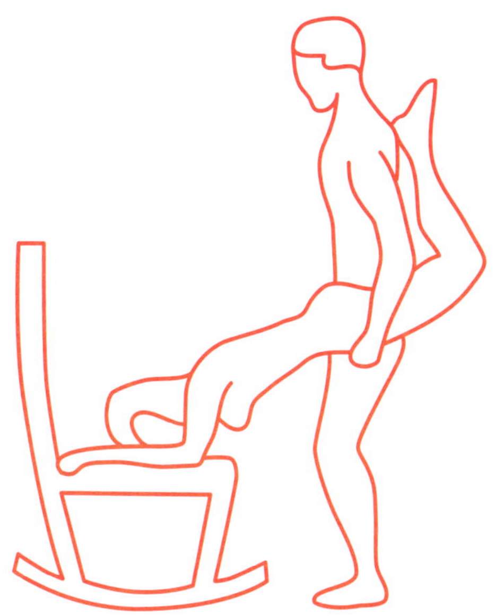

CALORIES

Giver 75.6

Receiver 54

EQUIPMENT

Rocking Chair

- ○ Below Average
- ○ Average
- ○ Above Average
- ○ Whoa!

COMMENTS

JULY 24)
THE JIGSAW PUZZLE

CALORIES

Giver 75.6

Receiver 48

- ○ Below Average
- ○ Average
- ○ Above Average
- ○ Whoa!

COMMENTS

JULY 25)

THE WISHBONE

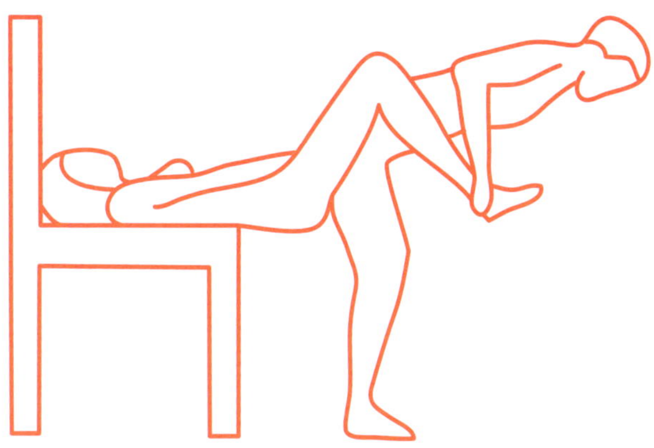

CALORIES

Giver 75.0

Receiver 54

EQUIPMENT

Chair

- ○ Below Average
- ○ Average
- ○ Above Average
- ○ Whoa!

COMMENTS

JULY 26)

THE WALLBANGER

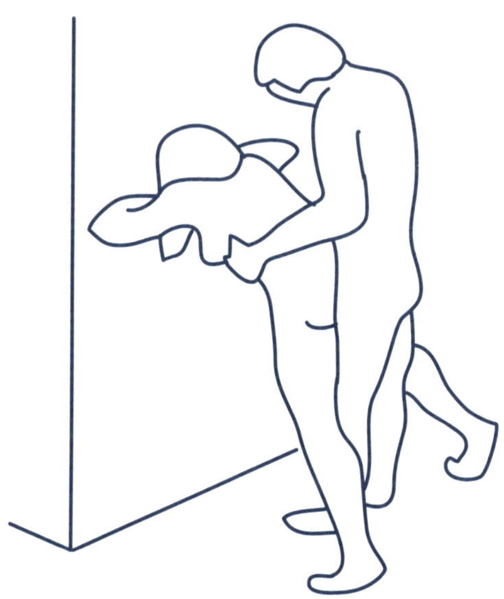

CALORIES

Giver 75.6

Receiver 54

EQUIPMENT

Wall

- ○ Below Average
- ○ Average
- ○ Above Average
- ○ Whoa!

COMMENTS

JULY 27)

WHAT THE CAT DRAGGED IN

CALORIES

Giver	134.4
Receiver	72

- ○ Below Average
- ○ Average
- ○ Above Average
- ○ Whoa!

COMMENTS

JULY 28)

THE BACKPACKER

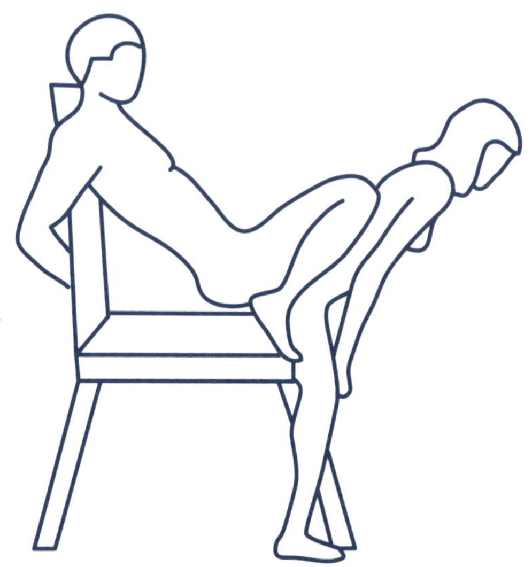

CALORIES

Giver 119.6

Receiver 48

EQUIPMENT

Chair

- ○ Below Average
- ○ Average
- ○ Above Average
- ○ Whoa!

COMMENTS

____

____

____

____

____

JULY 29)

THE “YOU MAY KISS THE BRIDE”

CALORIES

Giver 10.19

Receiver 13.6

EQUIPMENT

Pillow

- ○ Below Average
- ○ Average
- ○ Above Average
- ○ Whoa!

COMMENTS

JULY 30)

AURAL SEX

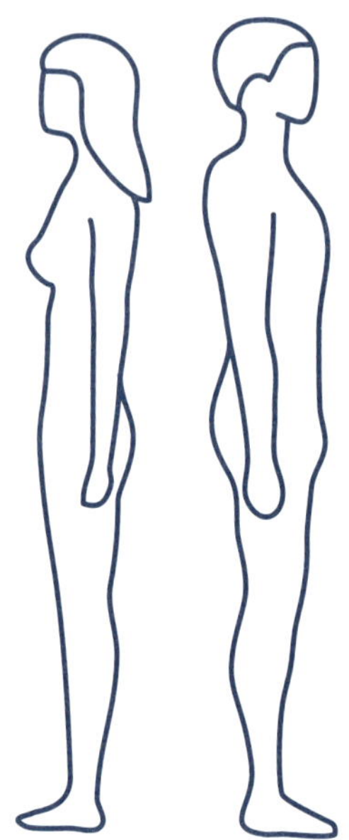

CALORIES

Giver	19
Receiver	13.6

HAZARD

Confusion
Loneliness

- ○ Below Average
- ○ Average
- ○ Above Average
- ○ Whoa!

COMMENTS

JULY 31)

THE CLOTHESLINE PIN

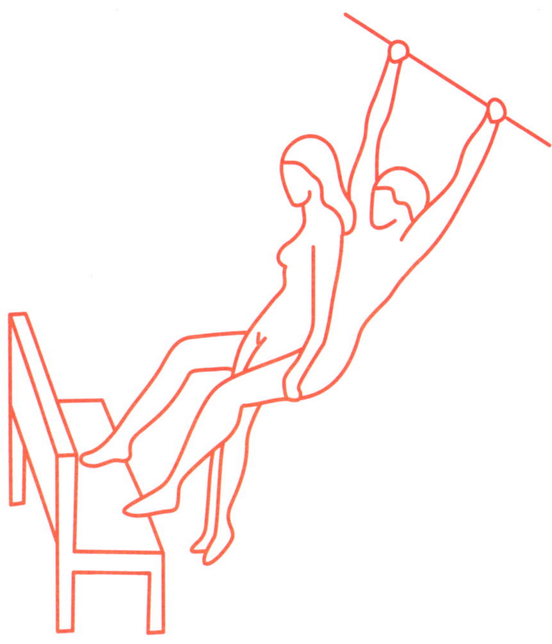

CALORIES		EQUIPMENT
Giver	104.4	Clothesline
Receiver	54	Bench

- ○ Below Average
- ○ Average
- ○ Above Average
- ○ Whoa!

COMMENTS

AUGUST 01)
THE DRAGONFLY

CALORIES

Giver 75.6

Receiver 96

- ○ Below Average
- ○ Average
- ○ Above Average
- ○ Whoa!

COMMENTS

AUGUST 02)

LAP OF LUXURY

CALORIES

Giver 48

Receiver 48

○ Below Average

○ Average

○ Above Average

○ Whoa!

COMMENTS

AUGUST 03)
ON A PEDESTAL

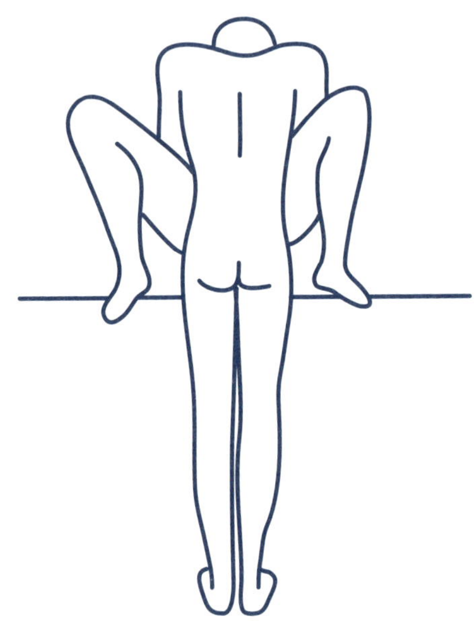

CALORIES
Giver 75.6
Receiver 54

EQUIPMENT
Table

- ○ Below Average
- ○ Average
- ○ Above Average
- ○ Whoa!

COMMENTS

AUGUST 04)

BEST FOOT FORWARD

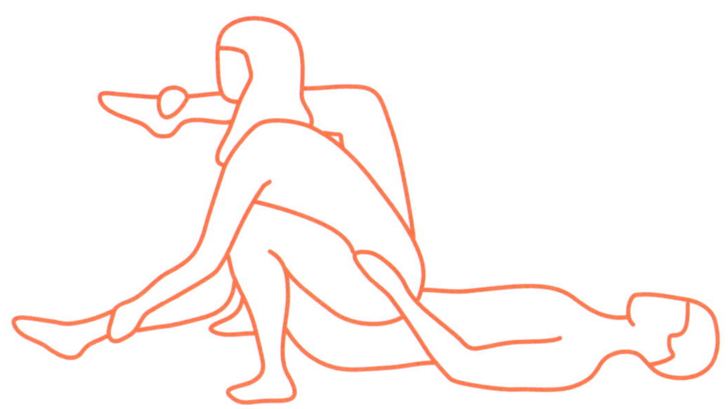

CALORIES

Giver 02

Receiver 49

- ○ Below Average
- ○ Average
- ○ Above Average
- ○ Whoa!

COMMENTS

AUGUST 05)
THE TIGHT SQUEEZE

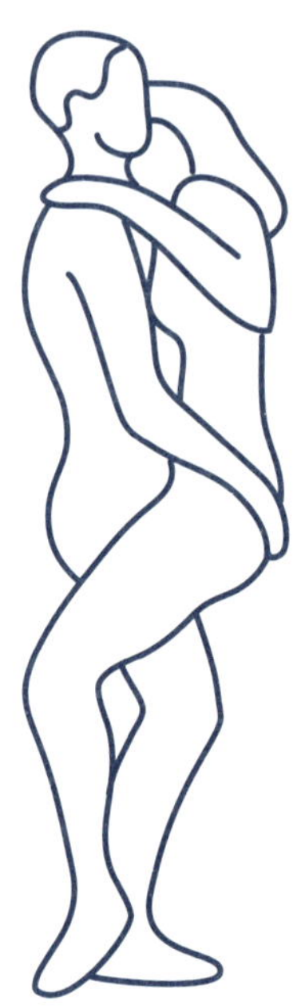

CALORIES

Giver 50.4

Receiver 54

- ○ Below Average
- ○ Average
- ○ Above Average
- ○ Whoa!

COMMENTS

AUGUST 06)

THE WALKING ON SUNSHINE

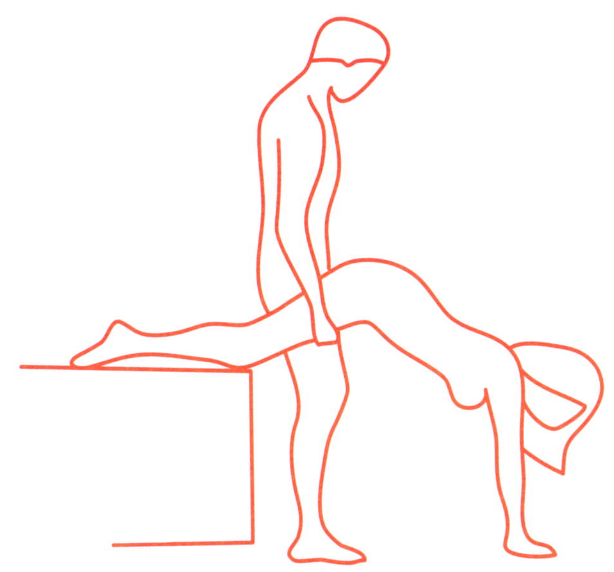

CALORIES

Giver 92.4

Receiver 96

EQUIPMENT

Bed

- ○ Below Average
- ○ Average
- ○ Above Average
- ○ Whoa!

COMMENTS

AUGUST 07)

KNOCKING ON HEAVEN'S DOOR

CALORIES

Giver 75.6

Receiver 66

EQUIPMENT

Doorframe

○ Below Average

○ Average

○ Above Average

○ Whoa!

COMMENTS

AUGUST 08)

THE WAKE-UP CALL

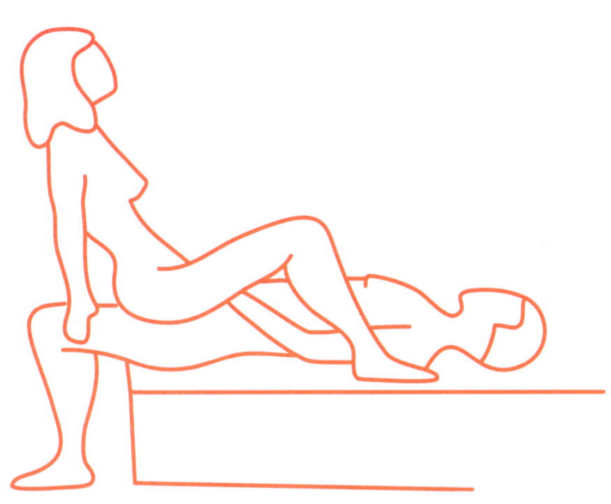

CALORIES

Giver 67.0

Receiver 54

EQUIPMENT

Bed

- ○ Below Average
- ○ Average
- ○ Above Average
- ○ Whoa!

COMMENTS

AUGUST 09)
ROCK WITH YOU

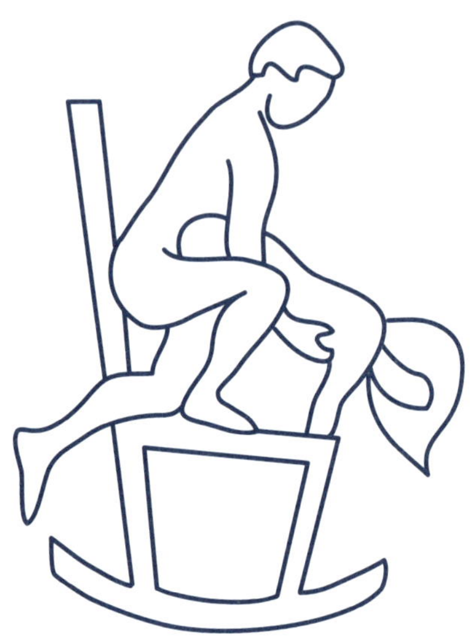

CALORIES

Giver	75.6
Receiver	54

EQUIPMENT

Rocking Chair

- ○ Below Average
- ○ Average
- ○ Above Average
- ○ Whoa!

COMMENTS

AUGUST 10)
THE GROIN VAULT

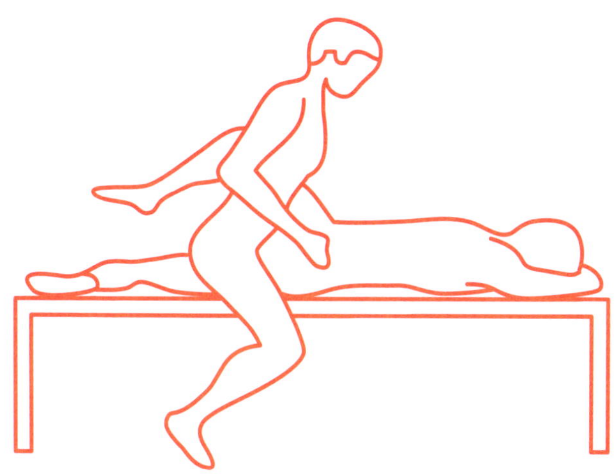

CALORIES		EQUIPMENT
Giver	75.6	Bench
Receiver	19	

- ○ Below Average
- ○ Average
- ○ Above Average
- ○ Whoa!

COMMENTS

AUGUST 11)
THE RUNNING WITH SCISSORS

CALORIES

Giver 75.6

Receiver 96

- ○ Below Average
- ○ Average
- ○ Above Average
- ○ Whoa!

COMMENTS

AUGUST 12)
THE BENCH PRESS

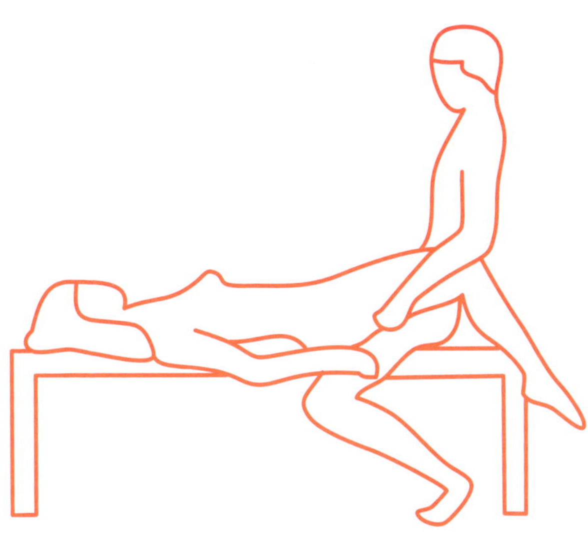

CALORIES
Giver 88
Receiver 54

EQUIPMENT
Bench

- ○ Below Average
- ○ Average
- ○ Above Average
- ○ Whoa!

COMMENTS

AUGUST 13)

REALLY HOT YOGA

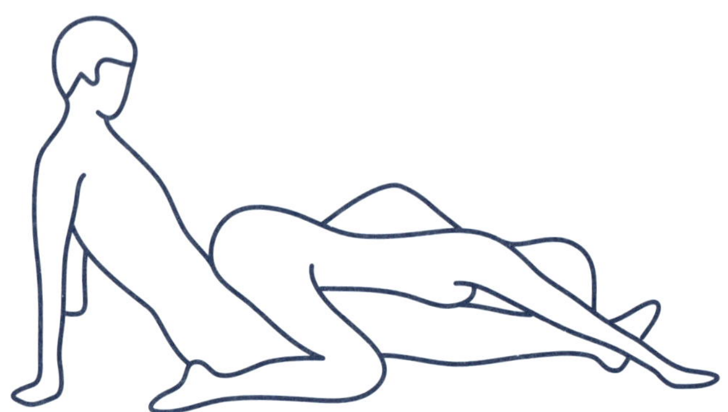

CALORIES

Giver 75.6

Receiver 48

- ○ Below Average
- ○ Average
- ○ Above Average
- ○ Whoa!

COMMENTS

AUGUST 14)

THE HEELS OVER HEAD

CALORIES	
Giver	134.4
Receiver	72

- ○ Below Average
- ○ Average
- ○ Above Average
- ○ Whoa!

COMMENTS

______

______

______

______

______

______

AUGUST 15)
THE BOTTOMS UP

CALORIES		EQUIPMENT	HAZARD	
Giver	67.2	Rocking Chair	Explaining Position to Partner	○ Below Average
Receiver	48	Ottoman		○ Average
				○ Above Average
				○ Whoa!

COMMENTS

AUGUST 16)

WEAK IN THE KNEES

CALORIES

Giver 67.2

Receiver 48

○ Below Average
○ Average
○ Above Average
○ Whoa!

COMMENTS

AUGUST 17)
THE ADVANCED FOOTSIE

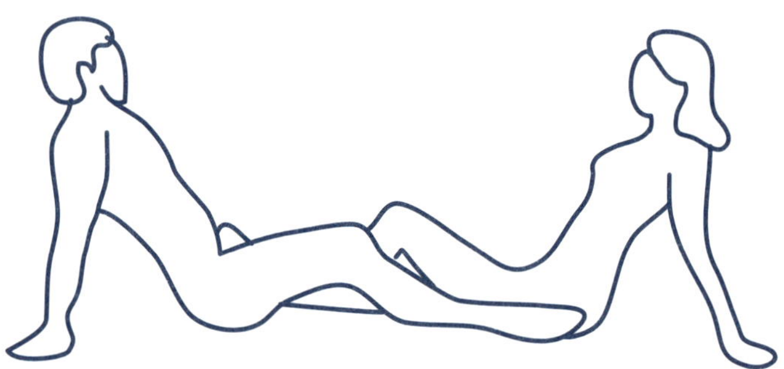

CALORIES
Giver 19
Receiver 13.6

EQUIPMENT
Optional:
Nail Clipper
Pumice Stone

HAZARD
Long Toenails

- ○ Below Average
- ○ Average
- ○ Above Average
- ○ Whoa!

COMMENTS

____
____
____
____
____
____

AUGUST 18)

THE FOUR ON THE FLOOR

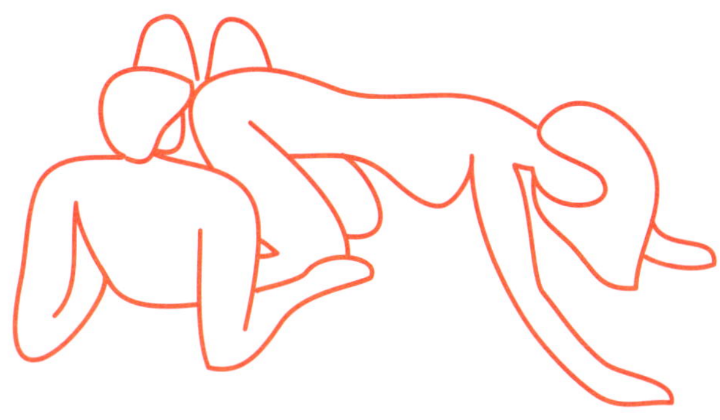

CALORIES

Giver	92.4
Receiver	66

- ○ Below Average
- ○ Average
- ○ Above Average
- ○ Whoa!

COMMENTS

AUGUST 19)

THE CHERRY ON TOP

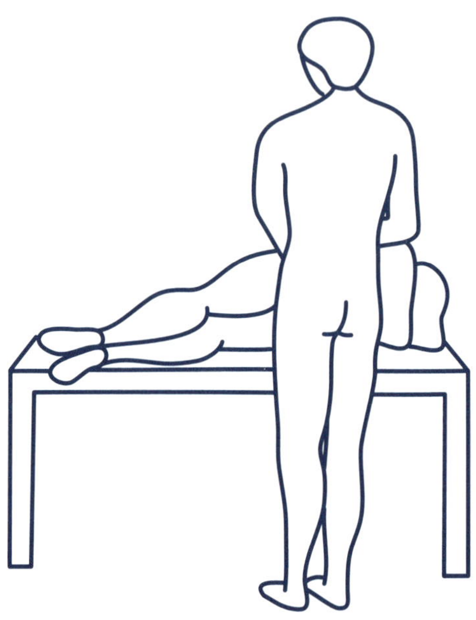

CALORIES

Giver 75.6

Receiver 54

EQUIPMENT

Table

- ○ Below Average
- ○ Average
- ○ Above Average
- ○ Whoa!

COMMENTS

AUGUST 20)
THE INSIDE VIEW

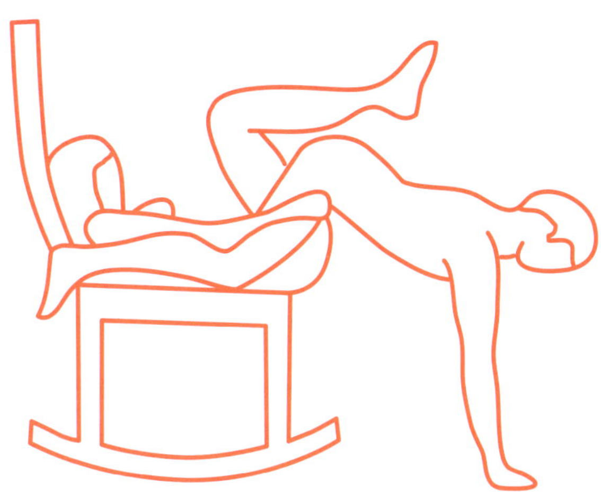

CALORIES
Giver 85
Receiver 54

EQUIPMENT
Rocking Chair

- ○ Below Average
- ○ Average
- ○ Above Average
- ○ Whoa!

COMMENTS

AUGUST 21)
THE BACK CRACKER

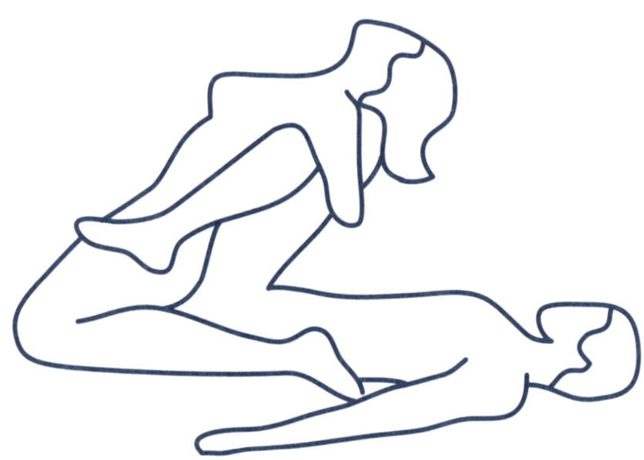

CALORIES

Giver 134.4

Receiver 96

- ○ Below Average
- ○ Average
- ○ Above Average
- ○ Whoa!

COMMENTS

AUGUST 22)
GETTING A LIFT

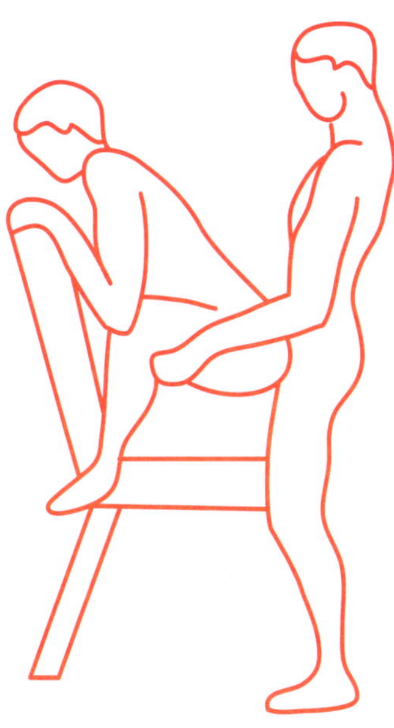

CALORIES		EQUIPMENT	
Giver	134	Chair	○ Below Average
Receiver	75.6		○ Average
			○ Above Average
			○ Whoa!

COMMENTS

AUGUST 23)
THE HERMIT CRAB

CALORIES

Giver 75.6

Receiver 54

- ○ Below Average
- ○ Average
- ○ Above Average
- ○ Whoa!

COMMENTS

AUGUST 24)

THE SOMETHING TO FALL BACK ON

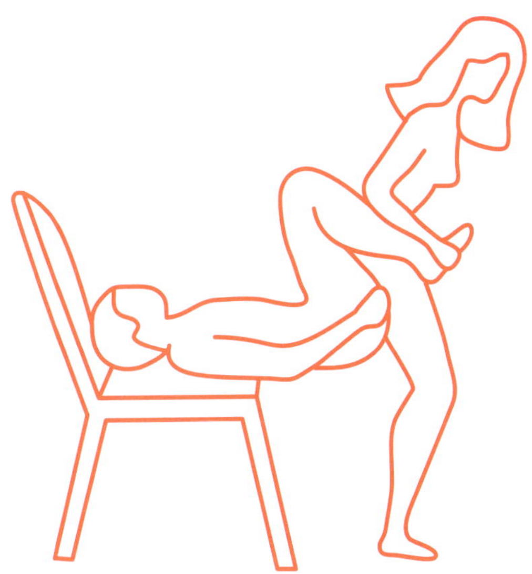

CALORIES		EQUIPMENT
Giver	67.2	Chair
Receiver	54	

- ○ Below Average
- ○ Average
- ○ Above Average
- ○ Whoa!

COMMENTS

AUGUST 25)

THE SWING DANCE

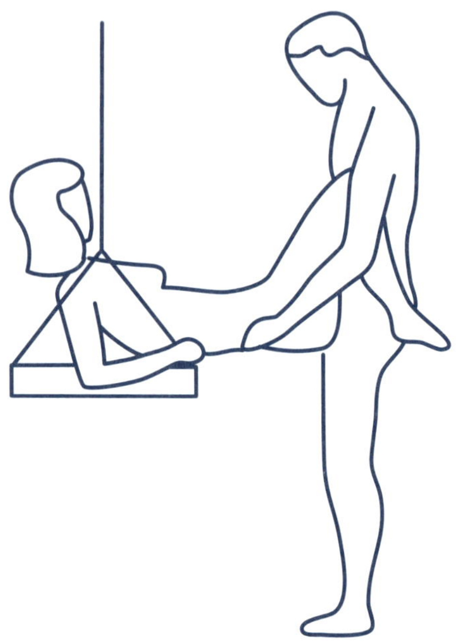

CALORIES

Giver 75.6

Receiver 66

EQUIPMENT

Porch Swing

- ○ Below Average
- ○ Average
- ○ Above Average
- ○ Whoa!

COMMENTS

AUGUST 26)
THE SIDE SPLITTER

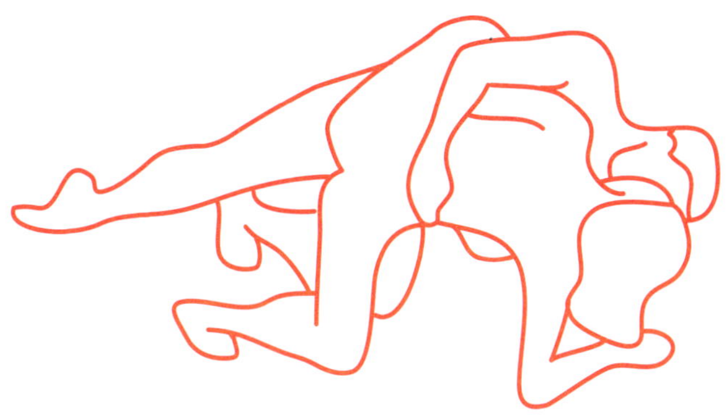

CALORIES

Giver 117.6

Receiver 54

- ○ Below Average
- ○ Average
- ○ Above Average
- ○ Whoa!

COMMENTS

AUGUST 27)
INNER PIECE

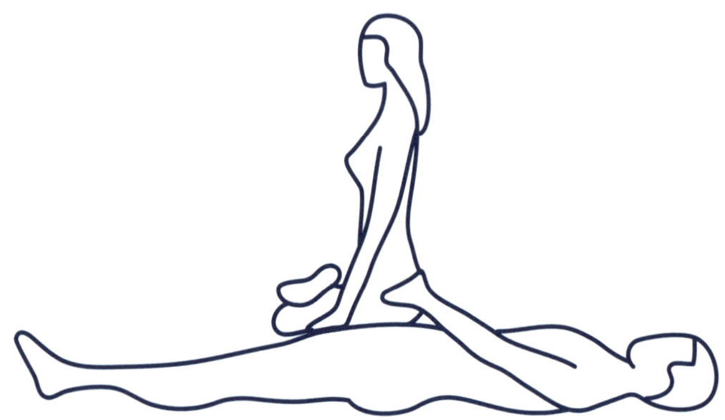

CALORIES

Giver 19

Receiver 54

BENEFIT

Enlightenment

- ○ Below Average
- ○ Average
- ○ Above Average
- ○ Whoa!

COMMENTS

AUGUST 28)

LEGS OVER EASY

CALORIES

Giver 75.6

Receiver 48

- ○ Below Average
- ○ Average
- ○ Above Average
- ○ Whoa!

COMMENTS

____

____

____

____

____

____

AUGUST 29)
THE SHAPE OF YOU

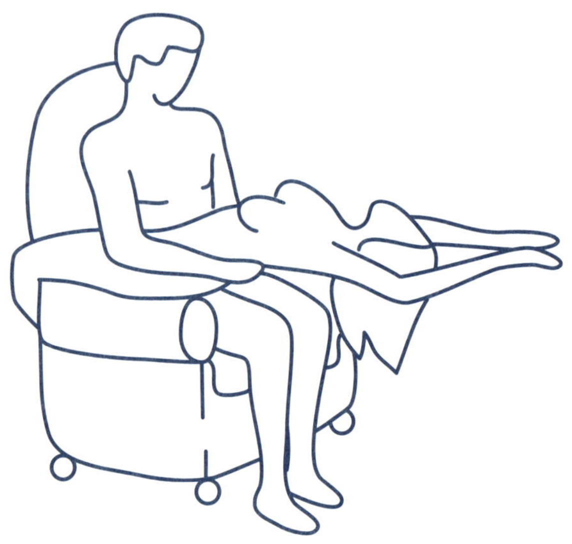

CALORIES
Giver 54
Receiver 63

EQUIPMENT
Chair

○ Below Average
○ Average
○ Above Average
○ Whoa!

COMMENTS

AUGUST 30)
THE GOOD SPANKING

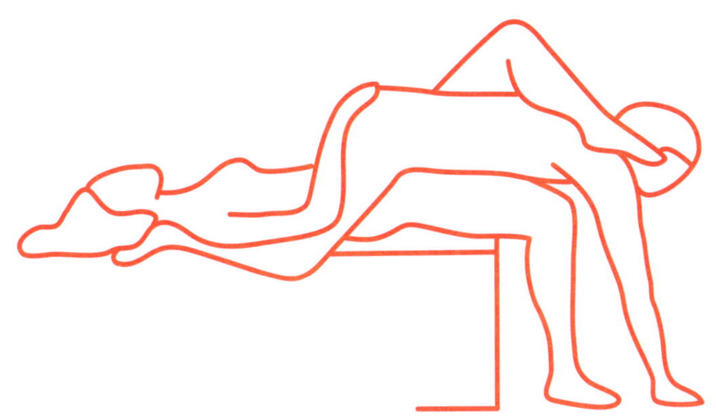

CALORIES		EQUIPMENT
Giver	67.2	Bed
Receiver	48	

○ Below Average
○ Average
○ Above Average
○ Whoa!

COMMENTS

AUGUST 31)

THE PICK ME UP

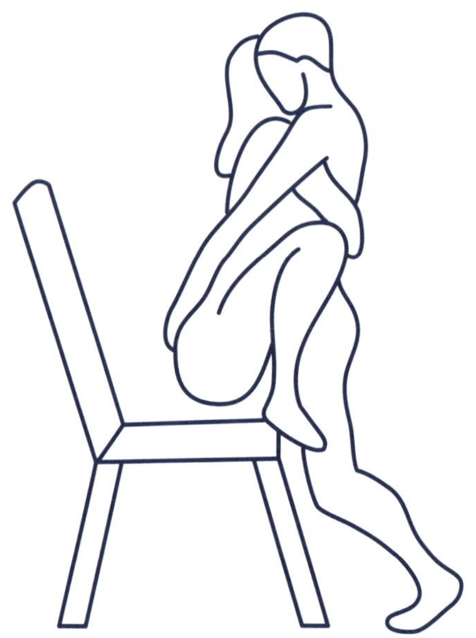

CALORIES

Giver 94

Receiver 57

EQUIPMENT

Chair

- ○ Below Average
- ○ Average
- ○ Above Average
- ○ Whoa!

COMMENTS

SEPTEMBER 01)

THE RUNNER'S KNEE

CALORIES	
Giver	75.6
Receiver	54

○ Below Average
○ Average
○ Above Average
○ Whoa!

COMMENTS

SEPTEMBER 02)

THE IMPROVIZED BED

CALORIES

Giver 37

Receiver 61

EQUIPMENT

Two Chairs

- ○ Below Average
- ○ Average
- ○ Above Average
- ○ Whoa!

COMMENTS

SEPTEMBER 03)
A GENTLE RIBBING

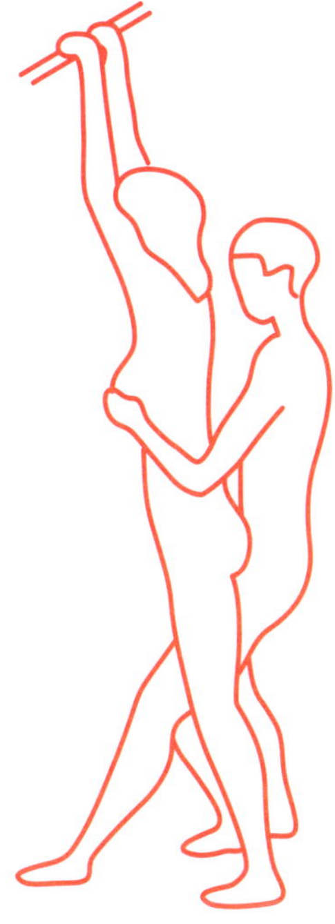

CALORIES

Giver 75.6

Receiver 66

EQUIPMENT

Pull-Up Bar

- ○ Below Average
- ○ Average
- ○ Above Average
- ○ Whoa!

COMMENTS

SEPTEMBER 04)
SHIFTING INTO DRIVE

CALORIES

Giver 45

Receiver 75

○ Below Average

○ Average

○ Above Average

○ Whoa!

COMMENTS

SEPTEMBER 05)
THE HEAD OVER HEELS

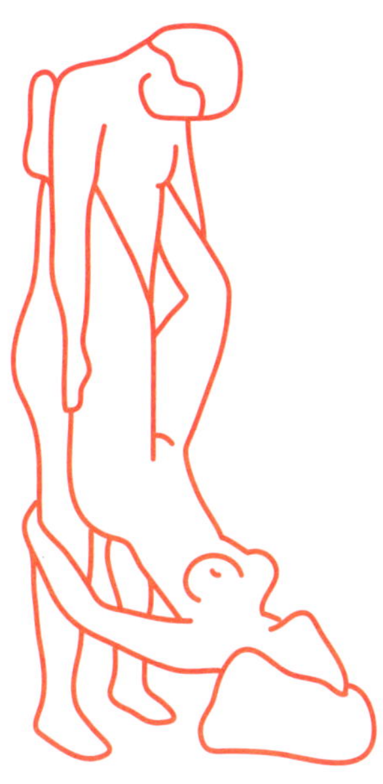

CALORIES

Giver 78

Receiver 45

○ Below Average
○ Average
○ Above Average
○ Whoa!

COMMENTS

SEPTEMBER 06)
THE LIFT FROM YOUR KNEES

CALORIES

Giver 98

Receiver 62

- ○ Below Average
- ○ Average
- ○ Above Average
- ○ Whoa!

COMMENTS

SEPTEMBER 07)

THE ROCK AND RIDE

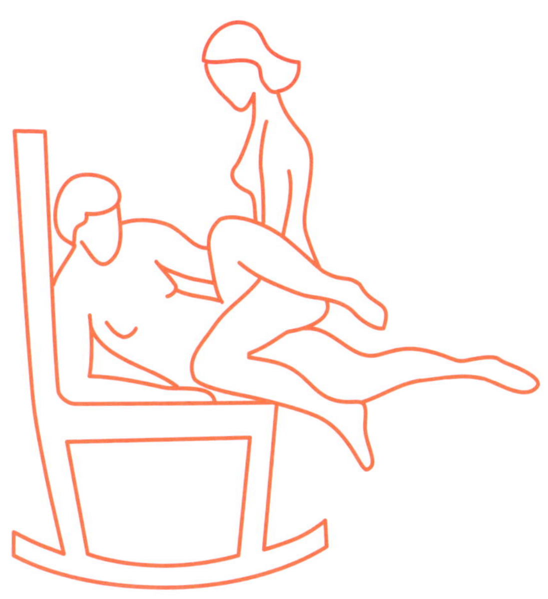

CALORIES

Giver 75.6

Receiver 58

EQUIPMENT

Rocking Chair

- ○ Below Average
- ○ Average
- ○ Above Average
- ○ Whoa!

COMMENTS

SEPTEMBER 08)
THE DOG ON THE PORCH

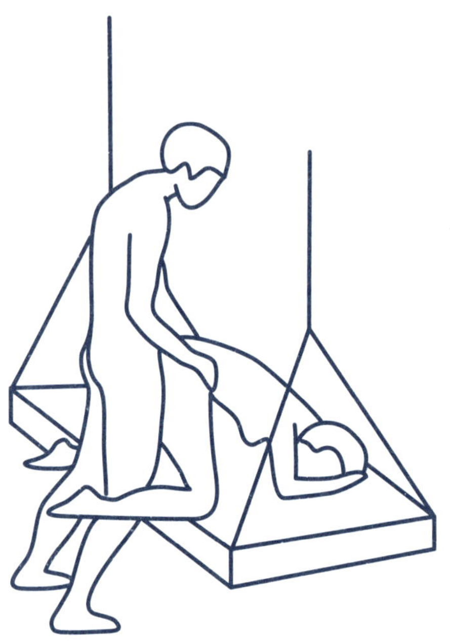

CALORIES

Giver 75.6

Receiver 66

EQUIPMENT

Porch Swing

○ Below Average

○ Average

○ Above Average

○ Whoa!

COMMENTS

SEPTEMBER 09)

THE "DROP ME AND I'LL SUE"

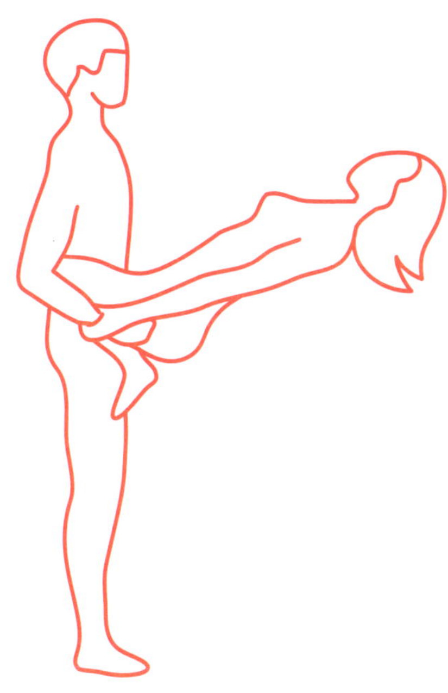

CALORIES

Giver 100.8

Receiver 132

EQUIPMENT

Lawyer

- ○ Below Average
- ○ Average
- ○ Above Average
- ○ Whoa!

COMMENTS

______

______

______

______

______

______

SEPTEMBER 10)

THE SQUEAKY WHEEL

CALORIES

Giver	67.2
Receiver	48

EQUIPMENT

Chair

Desk

- ○ Below Average
- ○ Average
- ○ Above Average
- ○ Whoa!

COMMENTS

SEPTEMBER 11)

THE HAPPY EXISTENTIALISTS

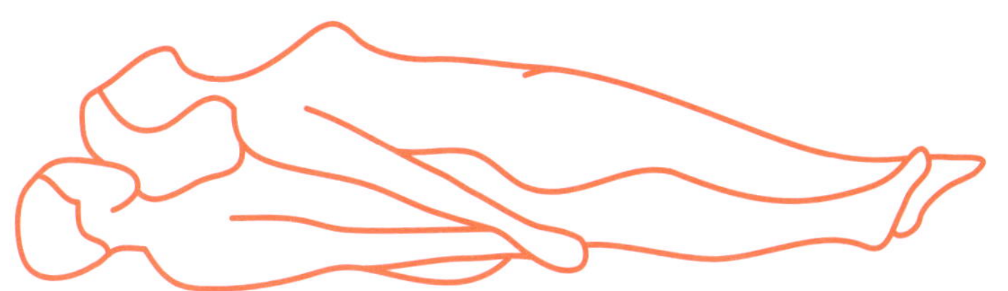

CALORIES

Giver	19
Receiver	23.6

- ○ Below Average
- ○ Average
- ○ Above Average
- ○ Whoa!

COMMENTS

SEPTEMBER 12)
THE HEDGE TRIMMER

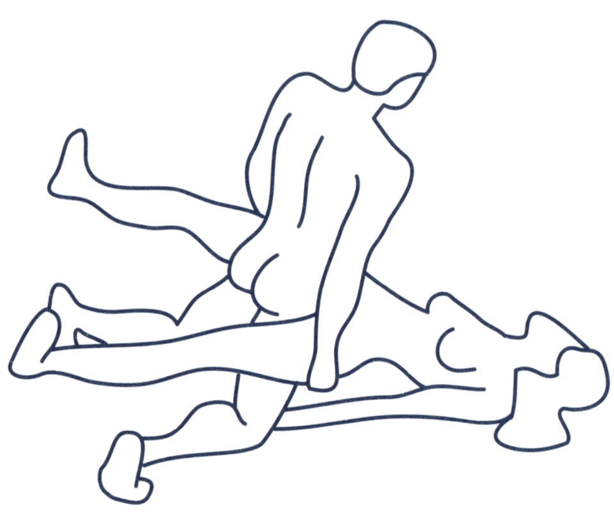

CALORIES

Giver 75.6

Receiver 13.6

- ○ Below Average
- ○ Average
- ○ Above Average
- ○ Whoa!

COMMENTS

SEPTEMBER 13)
THE "NOT SURE WE'RE DOING THIS RIGHT"

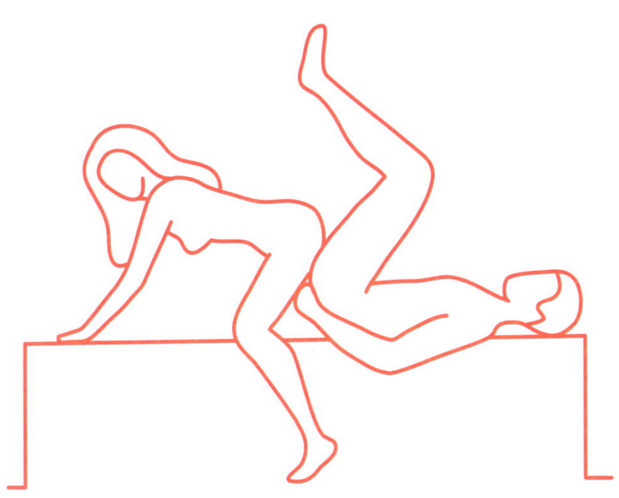

CALORIES		EQUIPMENT
Giver	75.6	Bench
Receiver	54	

- ○ Below Average
- ○ Average
- ○ Above Average
- ○ Whoa!

COMMENTS

SEPTEMBER 14)
THE BUNNY HILL

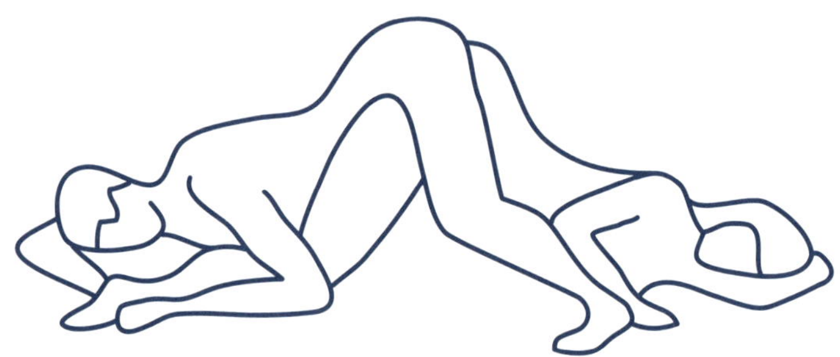

CALORIES

Giver 75.6

Receiver 54

- ○ Below Average
- ○ Average
- ○ Above Average
- ○ Whoa!

COMMENTS

SEPTEMBER 15)
THE "EX-CELLENT!"

CALORIES
Giver 19
Receiver 84

EQUIPMENT
Chair

- ○ Below Average
- ○ Average
- ○ Above Average
- ○ Whoa!

COMMENTS

SEPTEMBER 16)

ON YOUR MARK

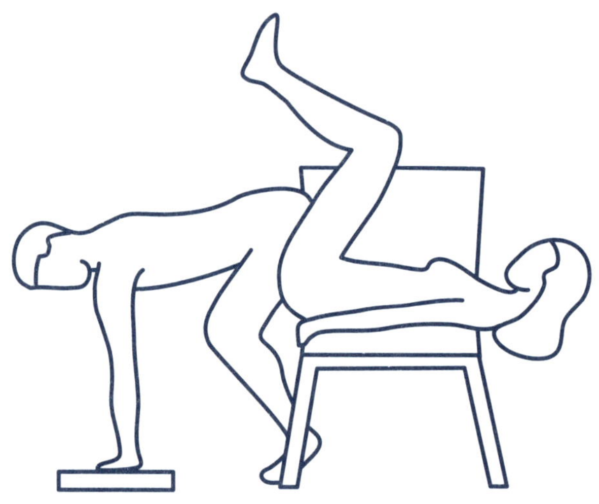

CALORIES

Giver 134.4

Receiver 96

EQUIPMENT

Chair

Stool

Optional: Start Gun

○ Below Average

○ Average

○ Above Average

○ Whoa!

COMMENTS

SEPTEMBER 17)

THE "WE SHOULD REALLY TALK"

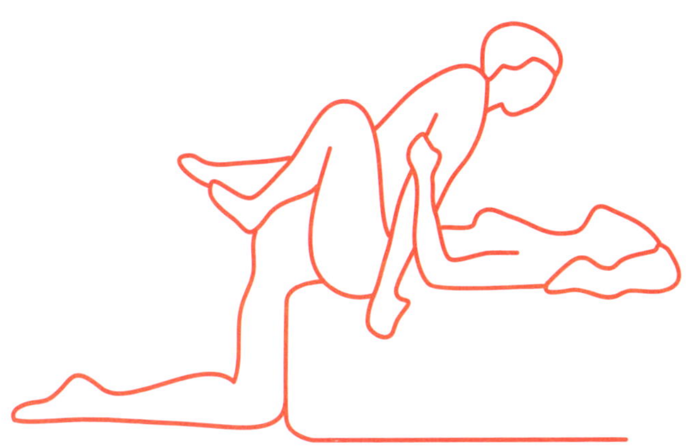

CALORIES

Giver 75.6

Receiver 48

EQUIPMENT

Bed

○ Below Average

○ Average

○ Above Average

○ Whoa!

COMMENTS

SEPTEMBER 18)

LICK MY NECK . . .

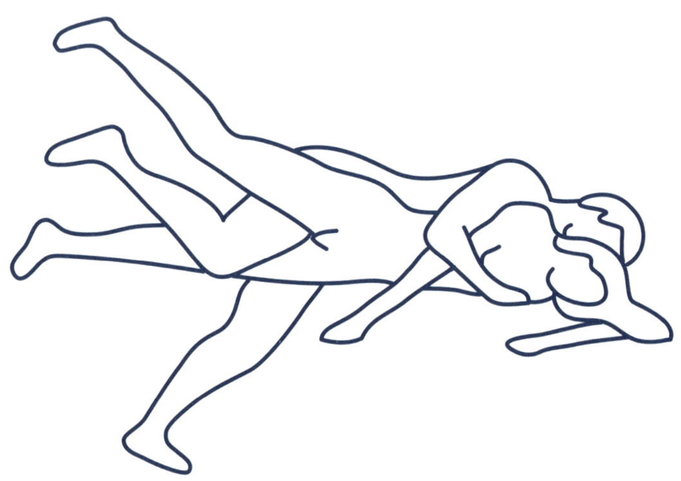

CALORIES

Giver 75

Receiver 66

- ○ Below Average
- ○ Average
- ○ Above Average
- ○ Whoa!

COMMENTS

SEPTEMBER 19)

THE "I GUESS THEY'RE RIGHT ABOUT FOOT SIZE AND . . ."

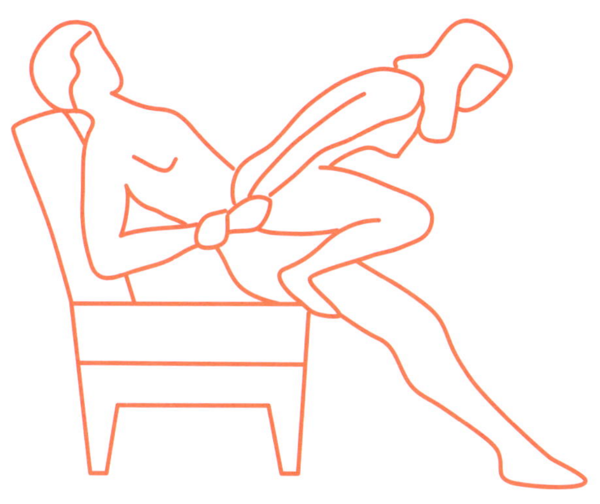

CALORIES		EQUIPMENT	
Giver	75.6	Nice Shoes	○ Below Average
Receiver	54	Chair	○ Average
			○ Above Average
			○ Whoa!

COMMENTS

____

____

____

____

____

____

SEPTEMBER 20)
IN YOUR CORNER

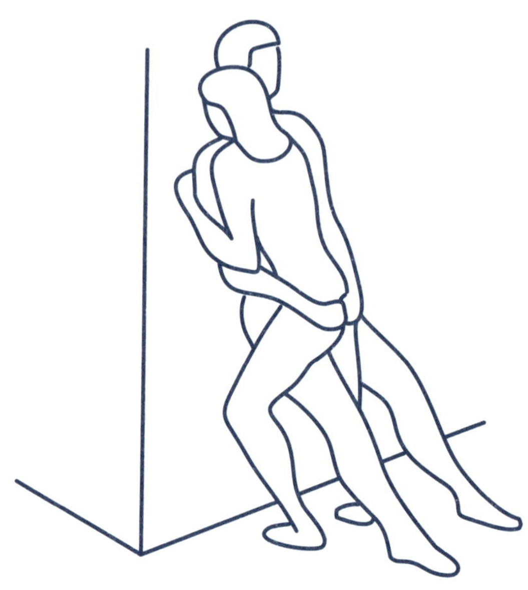

CALORIES

Giver	75.6
Receiver	54

EQUIPMENT

Wall

- ○ Below Average
- ○ Average
- ○ Above Average
- ○ Whoa!

COMMENTS

SEPTEMBER 21)
THE 7TH-INNING STRETCH

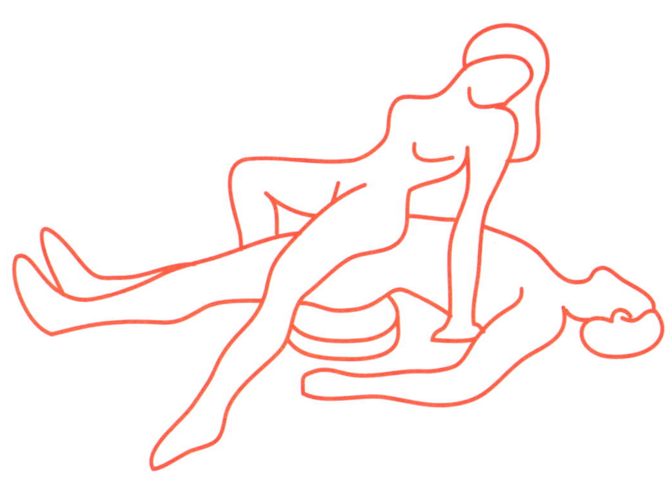

CALORIES
Giver 75.6
Receiver 96

EQUIPMENT
Pillow

- ○ Below Average
- ○ Average
- ○ Above Average
- ○ Whoa!

COMMENTS

SEPTEMBER 22)

RAISING THE BAR

CALORIES

Giver 75.6

Receiver 96

EQUIPMENT

Pull-Up Bar

○ Below Average

○ Average

○ Above Average

○ Whoa!

COMMENTS

SEPTEMBER 23)
THE BEDROOM SANDWICH

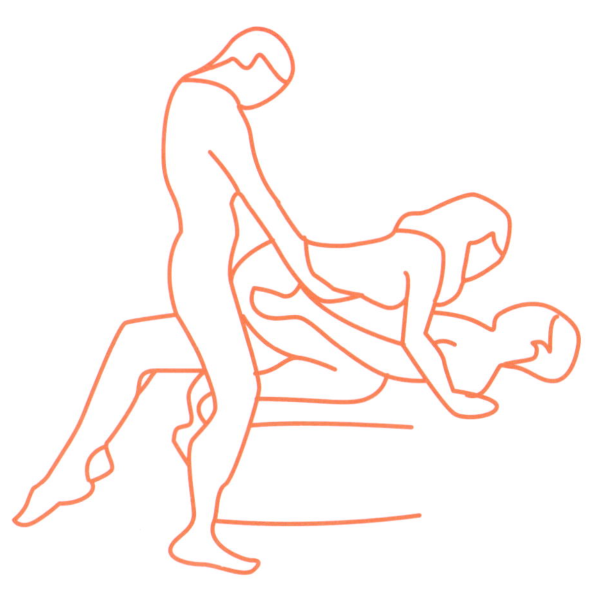

CALORIES		
Giver (Standing)	88	
Receiver	71	
Giver	73	

○ Below Average
○ Average
○ Above Average
○ Whoa!

COMMENTS

SEPTEMBER 24)
THE COORDINATES

CALORIES

Giver 100.8

Receiver 96

- ○ Below Average
- ○ Average
- ○ Above Average
- ○ Whoa!

COMMENTS

SEPTEMBER 25)

THE STAYCATION

CALORIES		EQUIPMENT	
Giver	67.2	Rocking Chair	○ Below Average
Receiver	54	Stool	○ Average
		Streaming Service	○ Above Average
			○ Whoa!

COMMENTS

SEPTEMBER 26)
THE GRAVITY CHECK

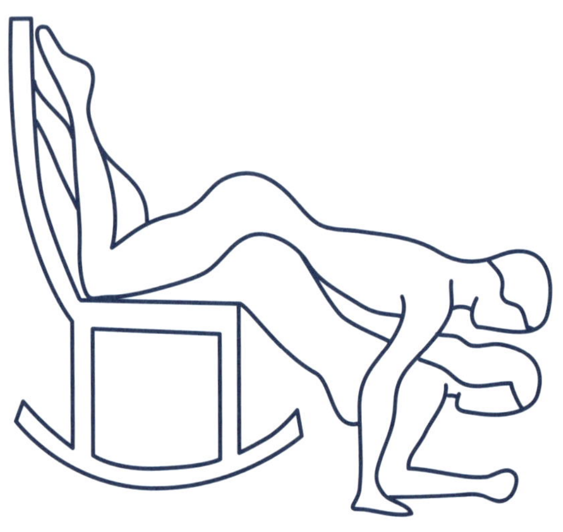

CALORIES		EQUIPMENT	HAZARD	
Giver	84	Rocking Chair	Sore Elbows	○ Below Average
Receiver	60			○ Average
				○ Above Average
				○ Whoa!

COMMENTS

SEPTEMBER 27)
THE CUDDLE BUG

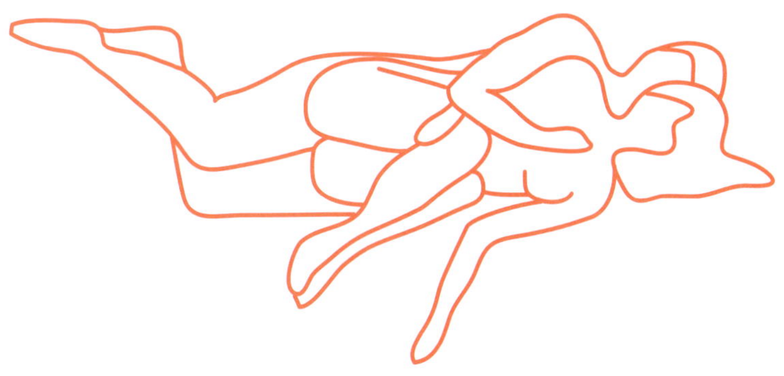

CALORIES

Giver 75.6

Receiver 95

- ○ Below Average
- ○ Average
- ○ Above Average
- ○ Whoa!

COMMENTS

____

____

____

____

____

____

SEPTEMBER 28)

THE CHARLIE HORSE

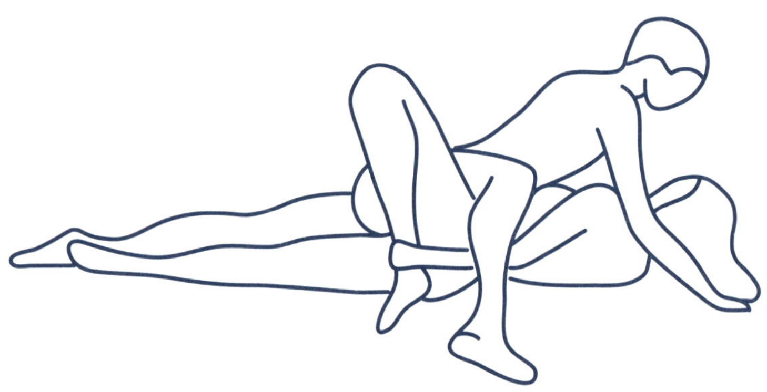

CALORIES

Giver 67.2

Receiver 48

- ○ Below Average
- ○ Average
- ○ Above Average
- ○ Whoa!

COMMENTS

SEPTEMBER 29)

THE UNDERSTUDY

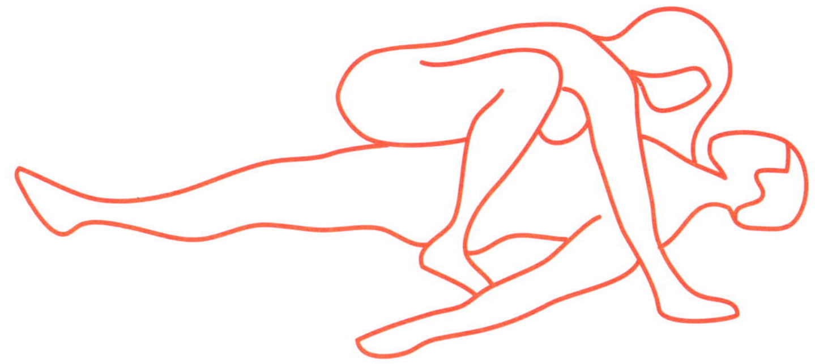

CALORIES

Giver 19

Receiver 54

○ Below Average

○ Average

○ Above Average

○ Whoa!

COMMENTS

SEPTEMBER 30)
THE WRESTLING MATCH

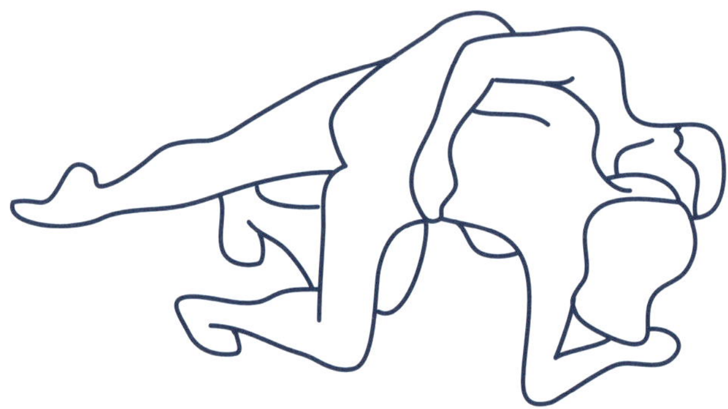

CALORIES

Giver 117.6

Receiver 54

- ○ Below Average
- ○ Average
- ○ Above Average
- ○ Whoa!

COMMENTS

OCTOBER 01)

THE HOT DOG AND A PRETZEL

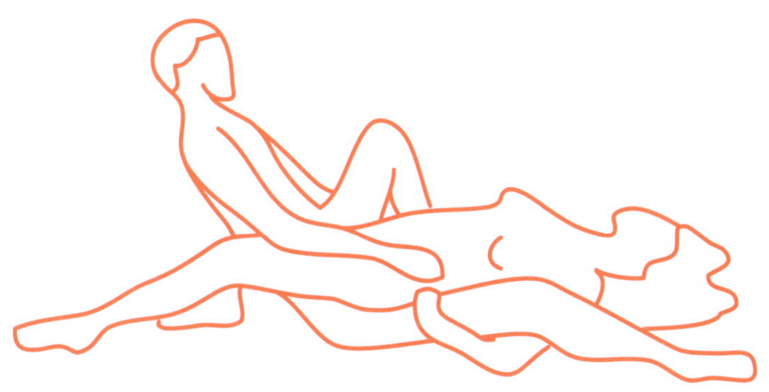

CALORIES

Giver 67

Receiver 49

- ○ Below Average
- ○ Average
- ○ Above Average
- ○ Whoa!

COMMENTS

OCTOBER 02)

A FOR EFFORT

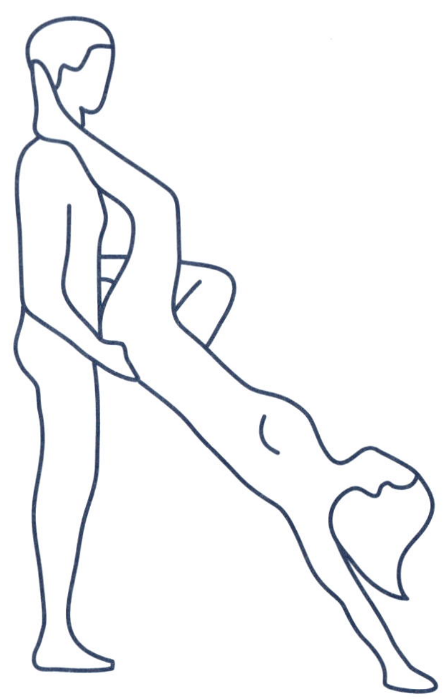

CALORIES

Giver 100.8

Receiver 96

- ○ Below Average
- ○ Average
- ○ Above Average
- ○ Whoa!

COMMENTS

OCTOBER 03)

THE BEND OVER BACKWARD

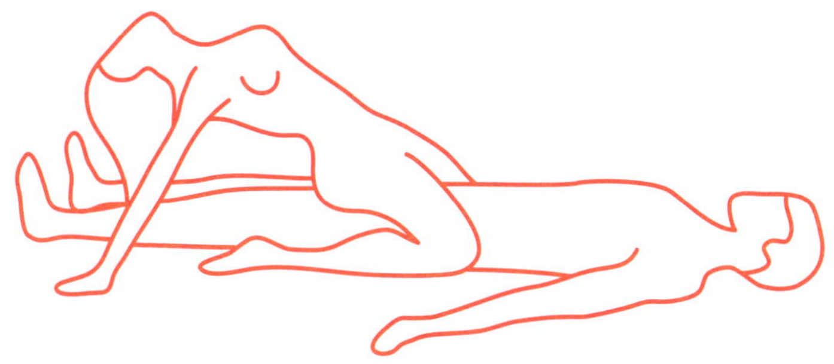

CALORIES	
Giver	67.2
Receiver	96

- ○ Below Average
- ○ Average
- ○ Above Average
- ○ Whoa!

COMMENTS

____

____

____

____

____

____

OCTOBER 04)

3-2-1 BLASTOFF

CALORIES

Giver 19

Receiver 54

- ○ Below Average
- ○ Average
- ○ Above Average
- ○ Whoa!

COMMENTS

OCTOBER 05)

THE "THAT'S AS FAR AS IT GOES"

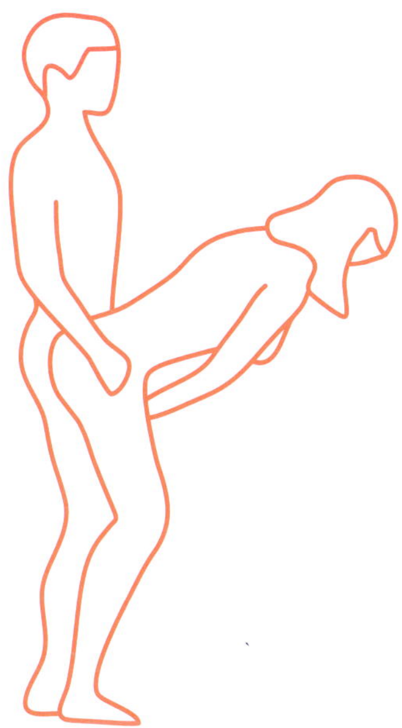

CALORIES

Giver	75.6
Receiver	54

- ○ Below Average
- ○ Average
- ○ Above Average
- ○ Whoa!

COMMENTS

OCTOBER 06)
THE SYNCHRONIZED SWIM

CALORIES

Giver 75.6

Receiver 54

- ○ Below Average
- ○ Average
- ○ Above Average
- ○ Whoa!

COMMENTS

OCTOBER 07)

THE SO CLOSE AND YET SO FAR

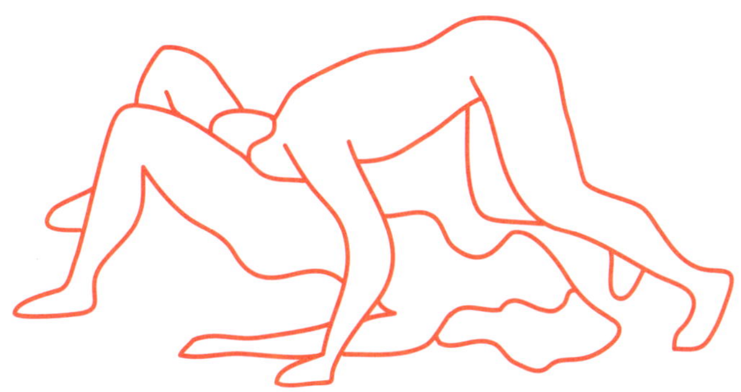

CALORIES

Giver 75.6

Receiver 96

- ○ Below Average
- ○ Average
- ○ Above Average
- ○ Whoa!

COMMENTS

OCTOBER 08)

THE LEAN INTO IT

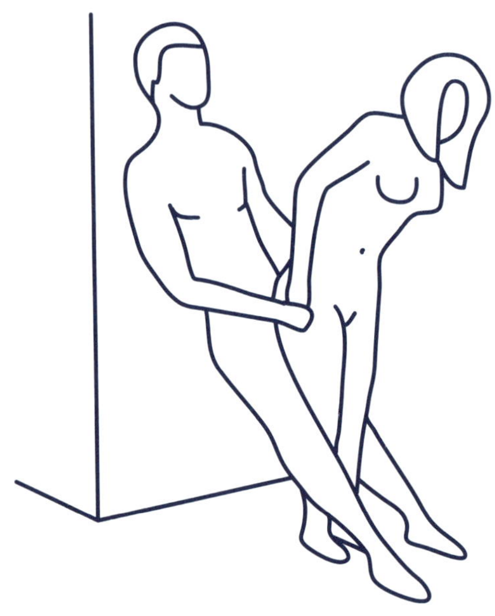

CALORIES

Giver 50.4

Receiver 54

EQUIPMENT

Wall

- ○ Below Average
- ○ Average
- ○ Above Average
- ○ Whoa!

COMMENTS

OCTOBER 09)
THE JOYRIDE

CALORIES

Giver	168
Receiver	48

- ○ Below Average
- ○ Average
- ○ Above Average
- ○ Whoa!

COMMENTS

OCTOBER 10)
THE ONE-NIGHT STAND

CALORIES
Giver 55
Receiver 60

EQUIPMENT
Chair

- ○ Below Average
- ○ Average
- ○ Above Average
- ○ Whoa!

COMMENTS

OCTOBER 11)

BOBBING FOR CHERRIES

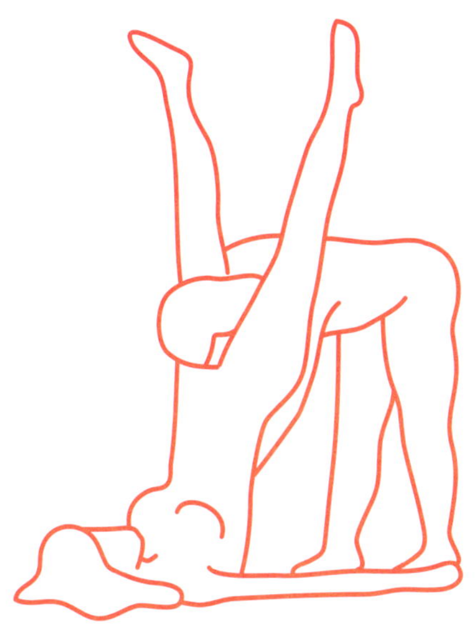

CALORIES	
Giver	54
Receiver	75.6

- ○ Below Average
- ○ Average
- ○ Above Average
- ○ Whoa!

COMMENTS

OCTOBER 12)

WAGGING THE DOG

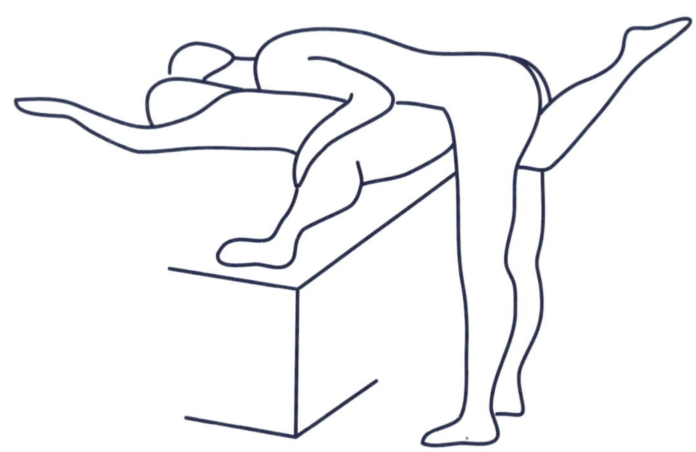

CALORIES

Giver 75.6

Receiver 66

EQUIPMENT

Bed

BENEFIT

Increased Flexibility

- ○ Below Average
- ○ Average
- ○ Above Average
- ○ Whoa!

COMMENTS

OCTOBER 13)
THE AFTERNOON DELIGHT

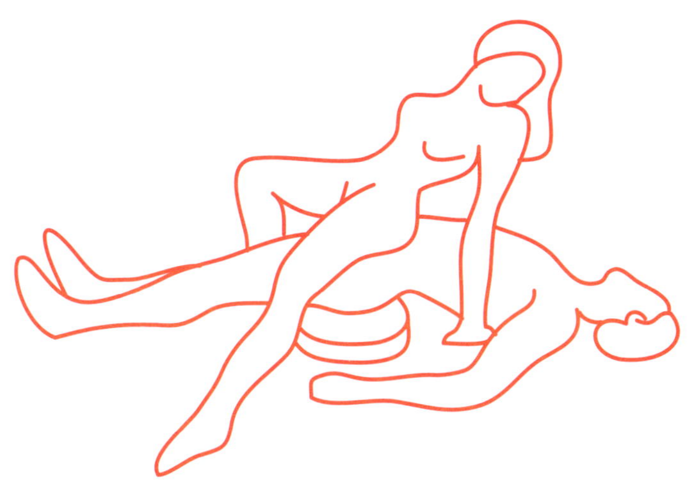

CALORIES		EQUIPMENT
Giver	75.6	Pillow
Receiver	96	

- ○ Below Average
- ○ Average
- ○ Above Average
- ○ Whoa!

COMMENTS

OCTOBER 14)
THE TONGUE IN CHEEK

CALORIES

Giver 13.6

Receiver 48

EQUIPMENT

Bed

- ○ Below Average
- ○ Average
- ○ Above Average
- ○ Whoa!

COMMENTS

OCTOBER 15)

THE SUNDAY PAPER

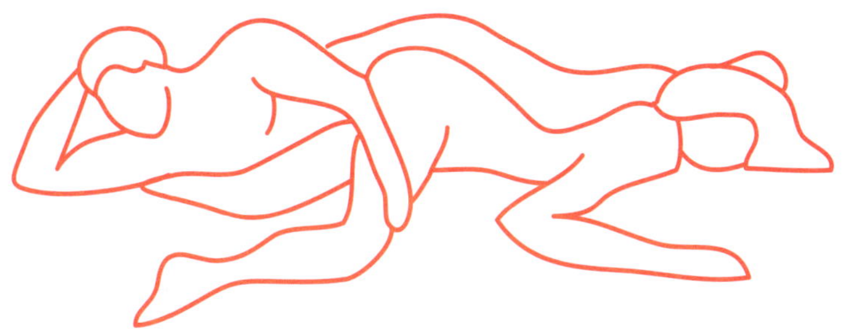

CALORIES		EQUIPMENT	
Giver	67.2	Newspaper	○ Below Average
Receiver	48		○ Average
			○ Above Average
			○ Whoa!

COMMENTS

____

____

____

____

____

____

OCTOBER 16)
THE HOT SLIDE

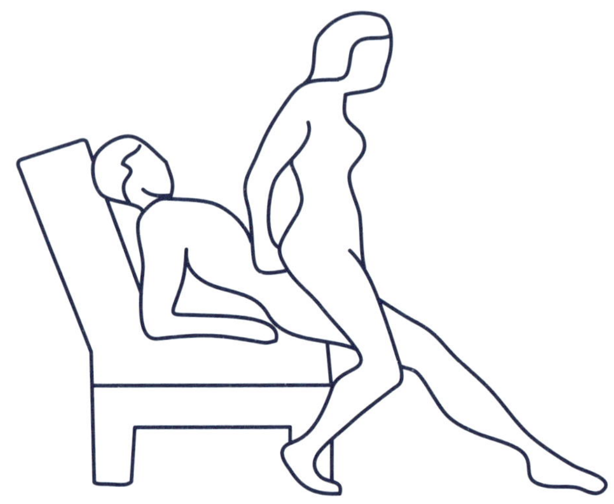

CALORIES		EQUIPMENT	HAZARD
Giver	75.6	Chair	Stop Immediately if You Hear a Snapping Sound
Receiver	54		

- ○ Below Average
- ○ Average
- ○ Above Average
- ○ Whoa!

COMMENTS

OCTOBER 17)

THE TRUST FALL

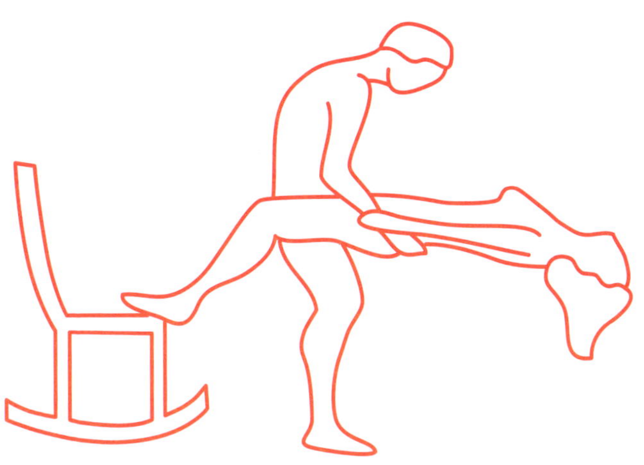

CALORIES		EQUIPMENT	BENEFIT	
Giver	117.6	Rocking Chair	New Sense of Trust in Relationship	○ Below Average
Receiver	84	Optional: Insurance		○ Average
				○ Above Average
				○ Whoa!

COMMENTS

OCTOBER 18)
THE HANG OF IT

CALORIES

Giver	134.4
Receiver	54

EQUIPMENT

Doorframe
Pull-Up Bar
Stool

○ Below Average
○ Average
○ Above Average
○ Whoa!

COMMENTS

OCTOBER 19)

THE FOOT WARMER

CALORIES

Giver 117.6

Receiver 96

- ○ Below Average
- ○ Average
- ○ Above Average
- ○ Whoa!

COMMENTS

OCTOBER 20)

THE DEN OF INIQUITY

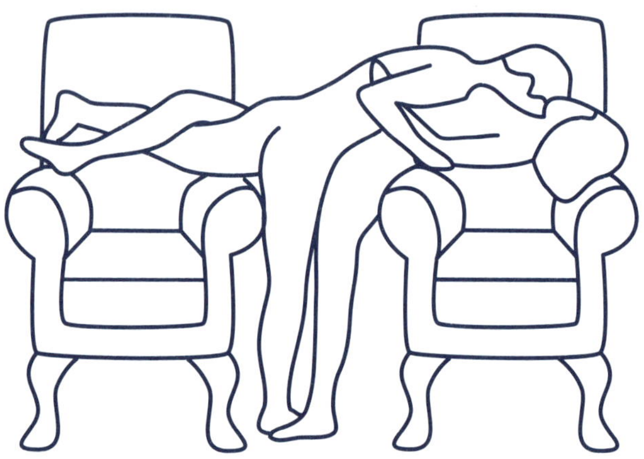

CALORIES

Giver 92.4

Receiver 84

EQUIPMENT

Two Chairs

- ○ Below Average
- ○ Average
- ○ Above Average
- ○ Whoa!

COMMENTS

OCTOBER 21)

THE HIP HUGGERS

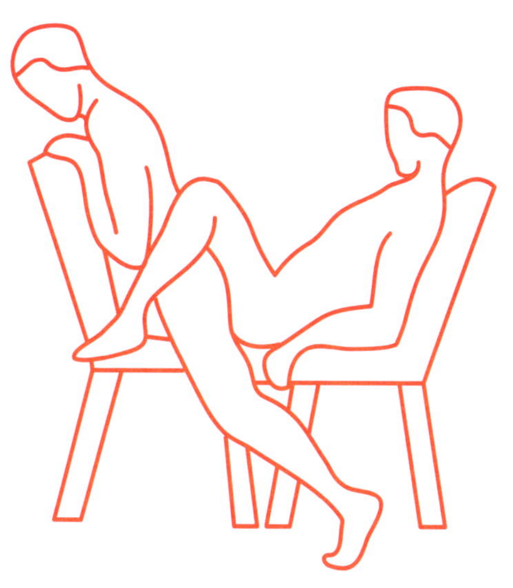

CALORIES

Giver 75.6

Receiver 66

EQUIPMENT

Two Chairs

- ○ Below Average
- ○ Average
- ○ Above Average
- ○ Whoa!

COMMENTS

OCTOBER 22)
THE "I'LL TAKE THE FRONT, YOU TAKE THE BACK"

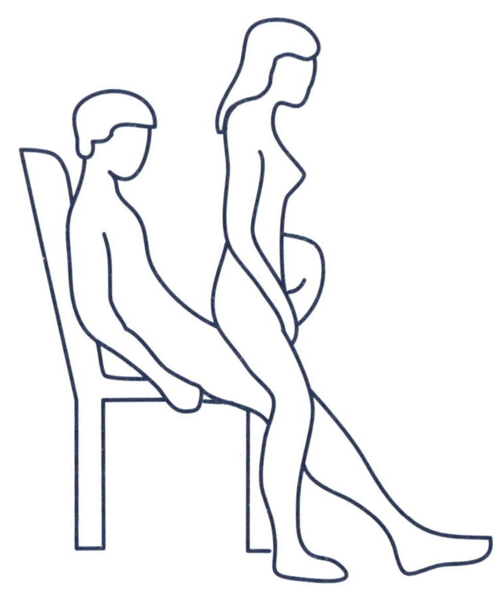

CALORIES

Giver 19

Receiver 84

EQUIPMENT

Chair

- ○ Below Average
- ○ Average
- ○ Above Average
- ○ Whoa!

COMMENTS

OCTOBER 23)
THE GOOD TASTE

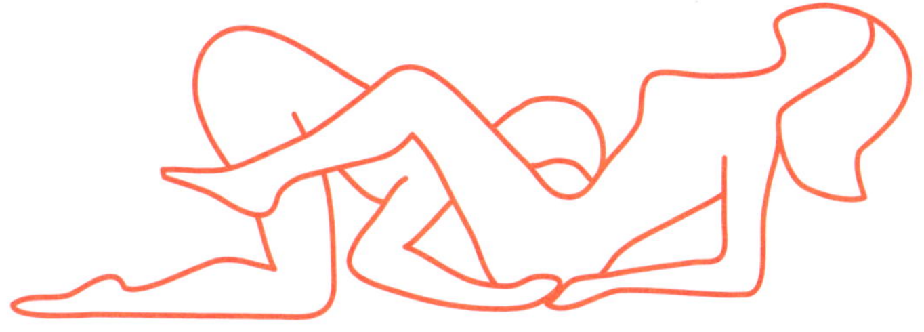

CALORIES

Giver 54

Receiver 19

- ○ Below Average
- ○ Average
- ○ Above Average
- ○ Whoa!

COMMENTS

OCTOBER 24)
K IS FOR KINKY

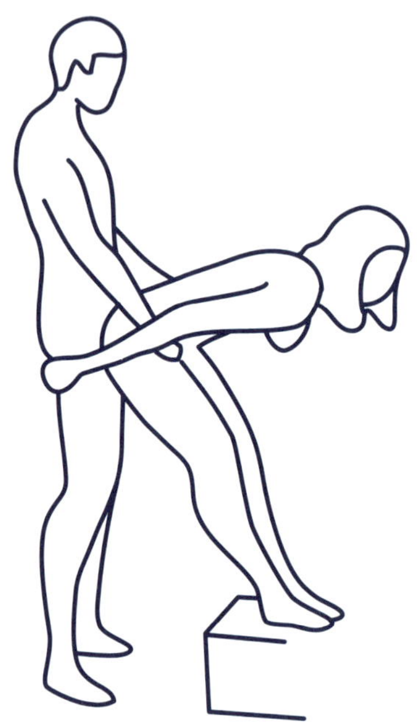

CALORIES

Giver 76.6

Receiver 54

EQUIPMENT

Stool

- ○ Below Average
- ○ Average
- ○ Above Average
- ○ Whoa!

COMMENTS

OCTOBER 25)
THE HANG SESH

CALORIES

Giver 13.6

Receiver 54

○ Below Average
○ Average
○ Above Average
○ Whoa!

COMMENTS

OCTOBER 26)

THE FACE PLANT

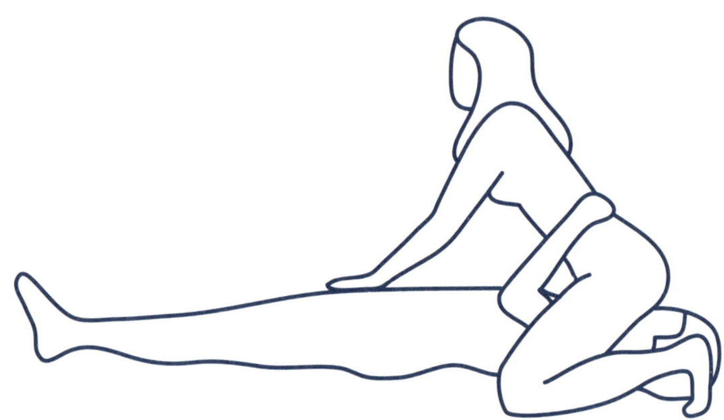

CALORIES

Giver 19

Receiver 48

- ○ Below Average
- ○ Average
- ○ Above Average
- ○ Whoa!

COMMENTS

OCTOBER 27)
THE GYROSCOPE

CALORIES

Giver	67.2
Receiver	54

EQUIPMENT

Rocking Chair

- ○ Below Average
- ○ Average
- ○ Above Average
- ○ Whoa!

COMMENTS

OCTOBER 28)
THE NEW PERSPECTIVE

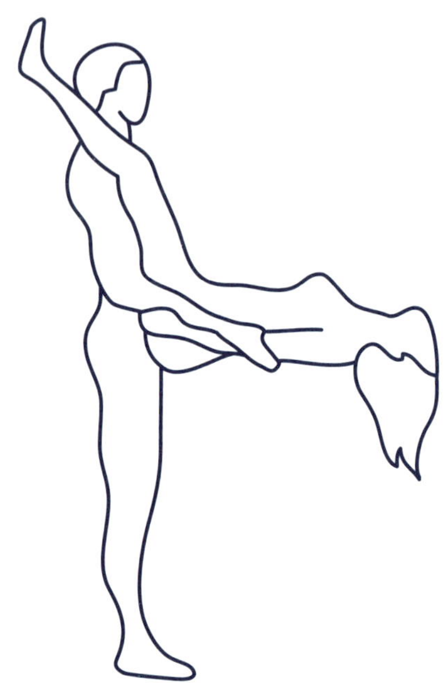

CALORIES

Giver 100.8

Receiver 96

○ Below Average
○ Average
○ Above Average
○ Whoa!

COMMENTS

OCTOBER 29)

"COULD YOU GRAB THE . . ."

CALORIES

Giver 50.4

Receiver 96

EQUIPMENT

Wall

- ○ Below Average
- ○ Average
- ○ Above Average
- ○ Whoa!

COMMENTS

OCTOBER 30)
THE FLYING TRAPEZE

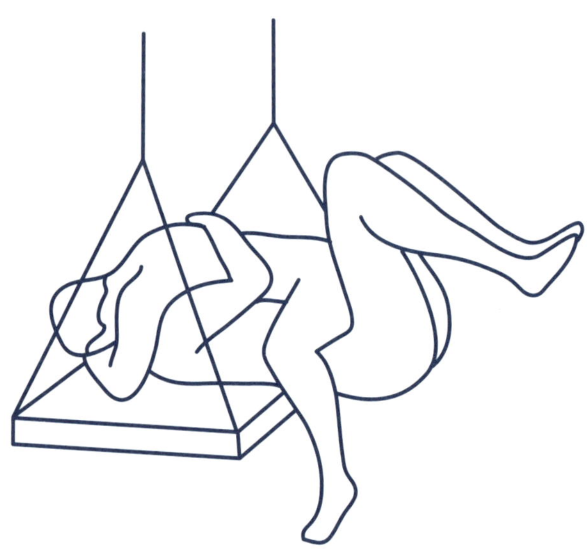

CALORIES

Giver	75.6
Receiver	66

EQUIPMENT

Swing

- ○ Below Average
- ○ Average
- ○ Above Average
- ○ Whoa!

COMMENTS

OCTOBER 31)

CARVING THE HALLOWEEN PUMPKIN

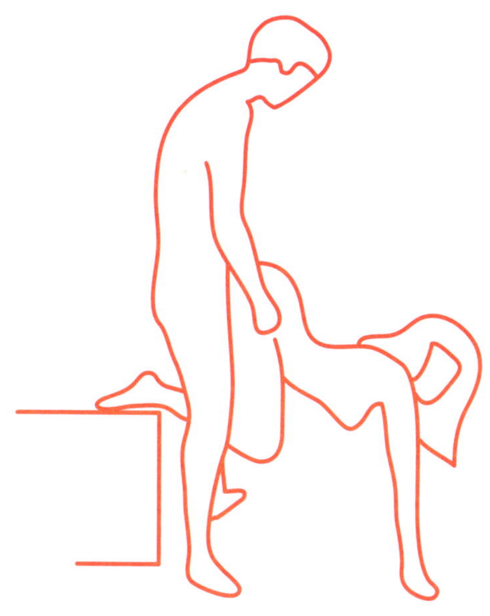

CALORIES

Giver 70

Receiver 62

EQUIPMENT

Bed

BENEFIT

No Costume Necessary

- ○ Below Average
- ○ Average
- ○ Above Average
- ○ Whoa!

COMMENTS

NOVEMBER 01)
THE "WEIRD FLEX, BUT OK"

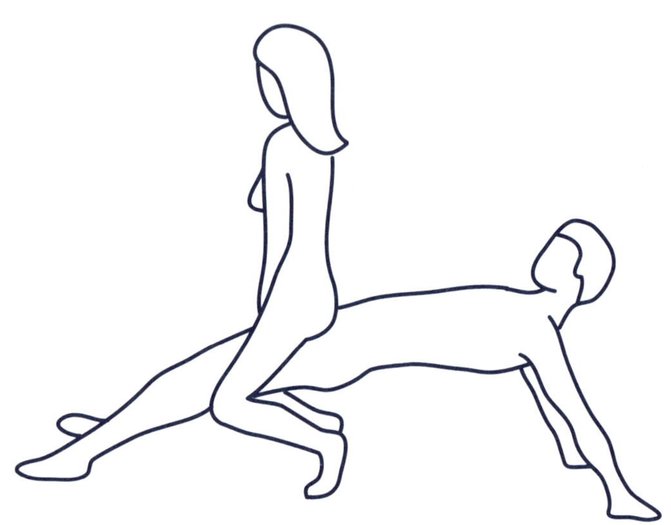

CALORIES

Giver 168

Receiver 54

- ○ Below Average
- ○ Average
- ○ Above Average
- ○ Whoa!

COMMENTS

NOVEMBER 02)

TIT FOR TAT

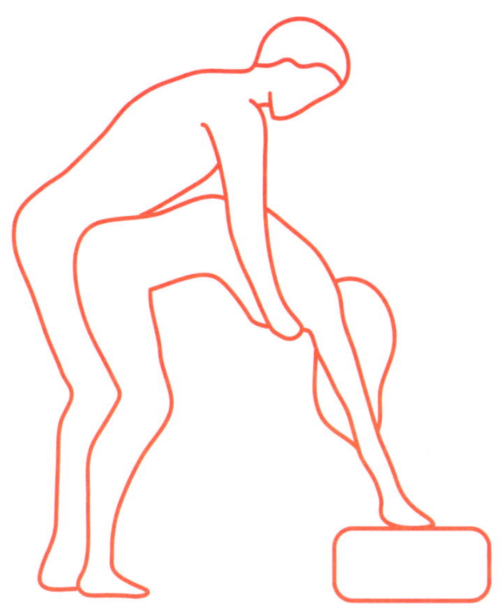

CALORIES

Giver 75.4

Receiver 56

EQUIPMENT

Stool

- ○ Below Average
- ○ Average
- ○ Above Average
- ○ Whoa!

COMMENTS

NOVEMBER 03)
THE TAKE IT EASY

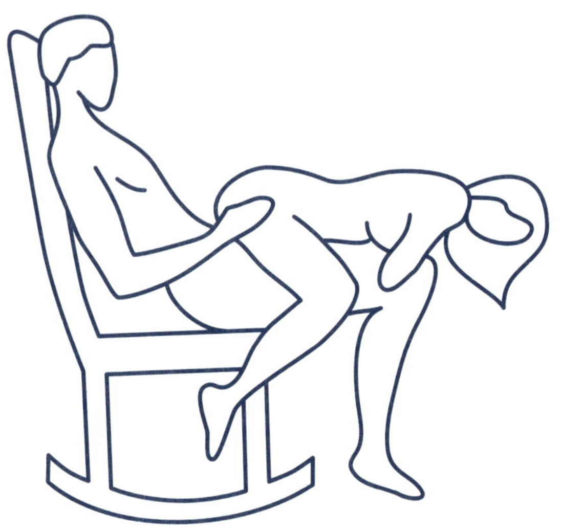

CALORIES
Giver 19
Receiver 54

EQUIPMENT
Rocking Chair

- ○ Below Average
- ○ Average
- ○ Above Average
- ○ Whoa!

COMMENTS

NOVEMBER 04)
THE ROWING MACHINE

CALORIES		EQUIPMENT
Giver	117.6	Rocking Chair
Receiver	118	

- ○ Below Average
- ○ Average
- ○ Above Average
- ○ Whoa!

COMMENTS

NOVEMBER 05)

ON POINTE

CALORIES

Giver 75.6

Receiver 92

EQUIPMENT

Bed

- ○ Below Average
- ○ Average
- ○ Above Average
- ○ Whoa!

COMMENTS

NOVEMBER 06)

SPEED DATING

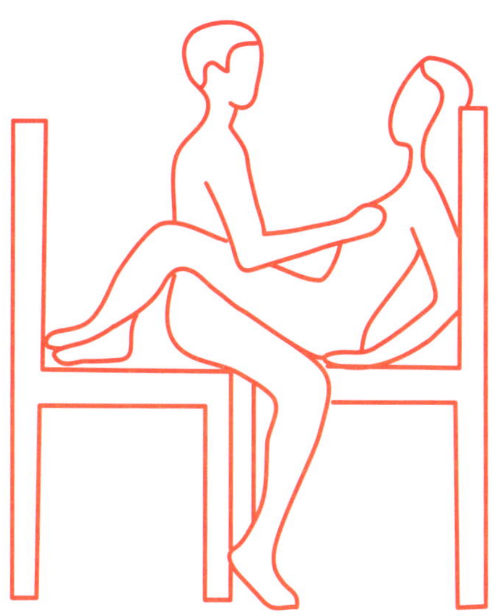

CALORIES		EQUIPMENT	HAZARD
Giver	37	Two Chairs	Fatigue
Receiver	61		

- ○ Below Average
- ○ Average
- ○ Above Average
- ○ Whoa!

COMMENTS

______

______

______

______

______

______

NOVEMBER 07)
HUT HUT HIKE

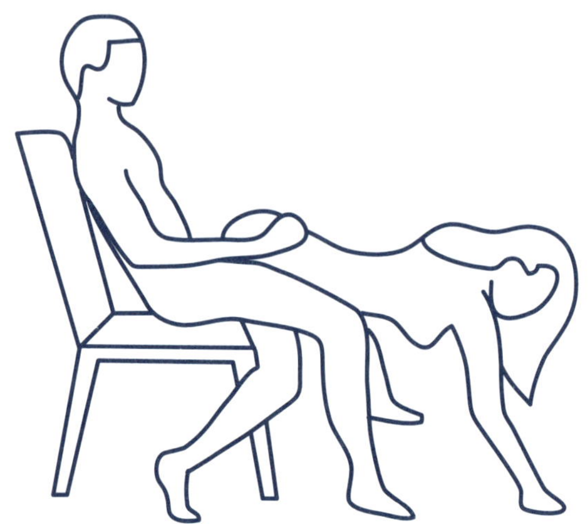

CALORIES
Giver 19
Receiver 48

EQUIPMENT
Chair
Optional: Helmets, Football Uniforms

HAZARD
Jock Strap

- ○ Below Average
- ○ Average
- ○ Above Average
- ○ Whoa!

COMMENTS

NOVEMBER 08)

THE "THIS JUST ISN'T WORKING OUT"

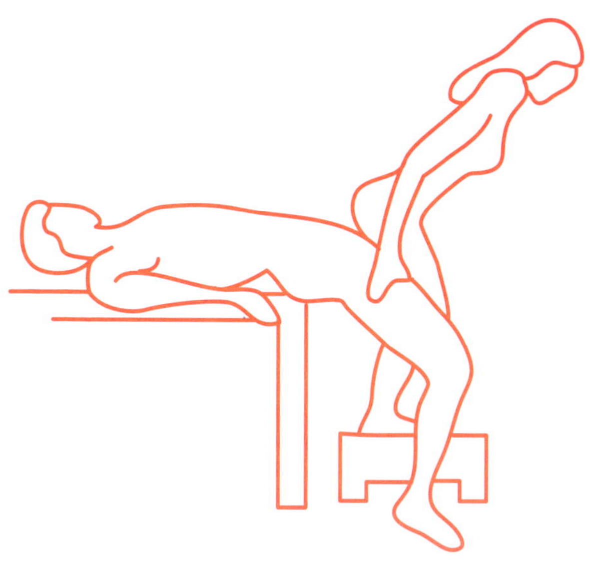

CALORIES

Giver 19

Receiver 120

EQUIPMENT

Table

Stool

HAZARD

Take All Things Before Leaving

- ○ Below Average
- ○ Average
- ○ Above Average
- ○ Whoa!

COMMENTS

____

____

____

____

____

____

NOVEMBER 09)

THE SLOW RIDE

CALORIES

Giver 75.6

Receiver 54

EQUIPMENT

Chair

- ○ Below Average
- ○ Average
- ○ Above Average
- ○ Whoa!

COMMENTS

NOVEMBER 10)
THE FLOAT YOUR BOAT

CALORIES

Giver	100.8
Receiver	132

- ○ Below Average
- ○ Average
- ○ Above Average
- ○ Whoa!

COMMENTS

NOVEMBER 11)

THE "SO, WHAT'S FOR DINNER?"

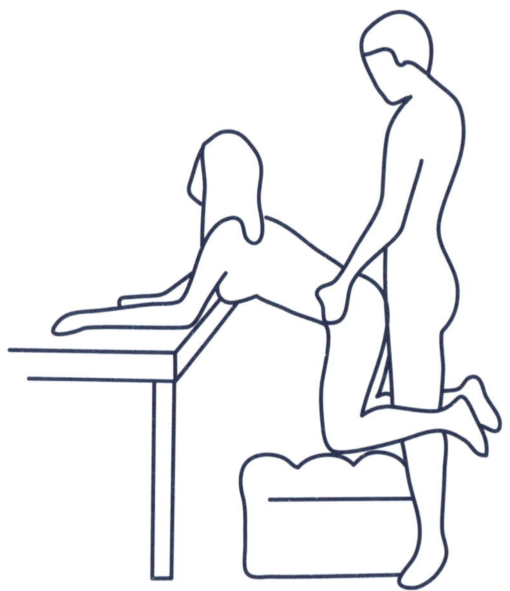

CALORIES

Giver 67.2

Receiver 48

EQUIPMENT

Table

Ottoman

- ○ Below Average
- ○ Average
- ○ Above Average
- ○ Whoa!

COMMENTS

NOVEMBER 12)
I CHAIR-ISH YOU

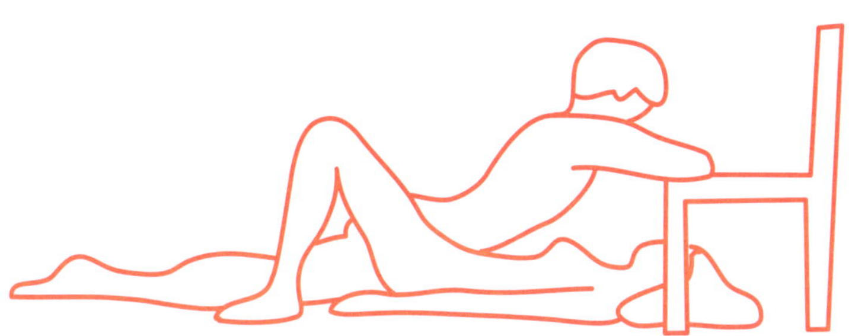

CALORIES
Giver 13.6
Receiver 67.2

EQUIPMENT
Chair

○ Below Average
○ Average
○ Above Average
○ Whoa!

COMMENTS

NOVEMBER 13)
THE LOUNGE ACT

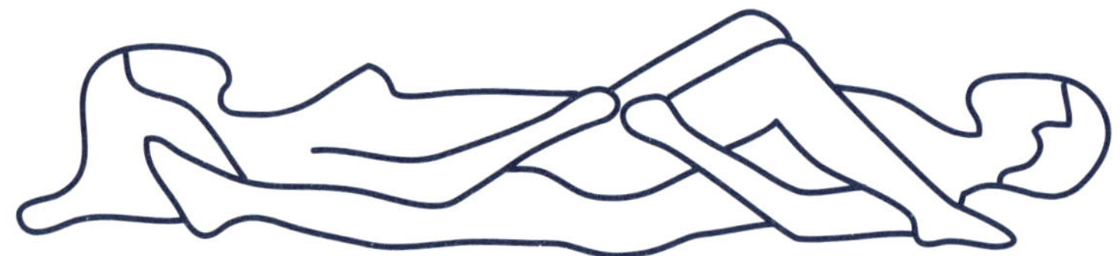

CALORIES

Giver 19

Receiver 13.6

HAZARD

Smelly Feet

- ○ Below Average
- ○ Average
- ○ Above Average
- ○ Whoa!

COMMENTS

NOVEMBER 14)
THE FANNY PACK

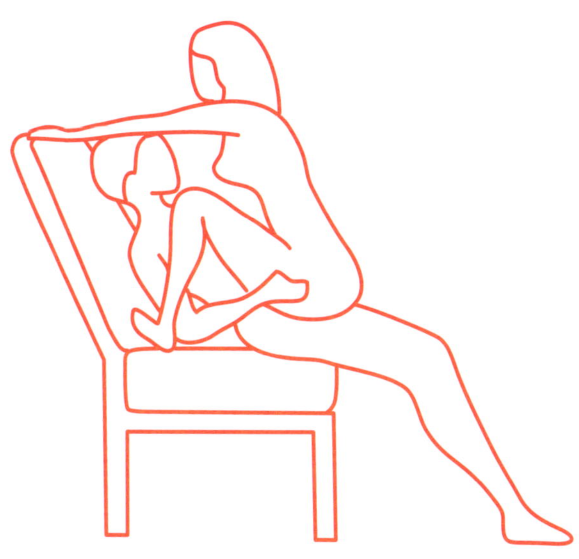

CALORIES

Giver 58

Receiver 65

EQUIPMENT

Chair

- ○ Below Average
- ○ Average
- ○ Above Average
- ○ Whoa!

COMMENTS

NOVEMBER 15)
FEAST MODE

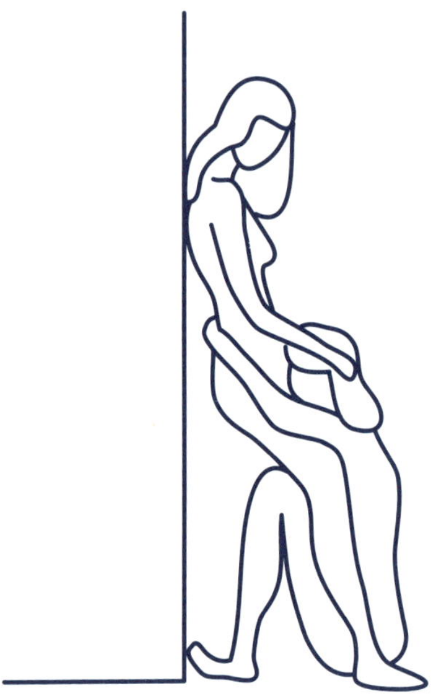

CALORIES

Giver 19

Receiver 13.6

EQUIPMENT

Wall

- ○ Below Average
- ○ Average
- ○ Above Average
- ○ Whoa!

COMMENTS

NOVEMBER 16)

THE HAND WARMER

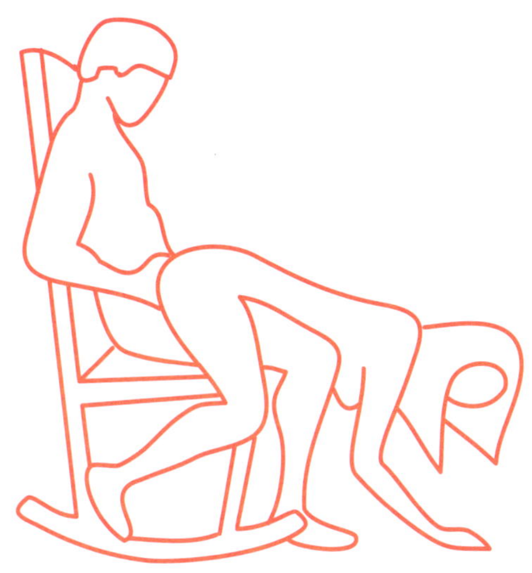

CALORIES

Giver 19

Receiver 60

EQUIPMENT

Rocking Chair

- ○ Below Average
- ○ Average
- ○ Above Average
- ○ Whoa!

COMMENTS

NOVEMBER 17)
THE "CAN I PLEASE TURN AROUND NOW?"

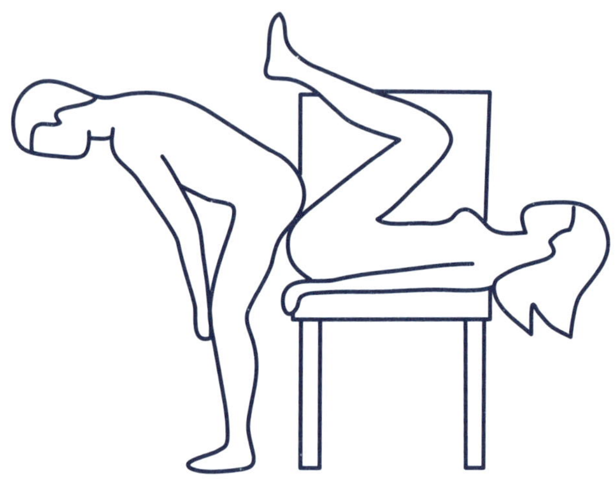

CALORIES

Giver 75.6

Receiver 54

EQUIPMENT

Chair

- ○ Below Average
- ○ Average
- ○ Above Average
- ○ Whoa!

COMMENTS

NOVEMBER 18)
THE STROKE OF GENIUS

CALORIES

Giver 35

Receiver 22

- ○ Below Average
- ○ Average
- ○ Above Average
- ○ Whoa!

COMMENTS

NOVEMBER 19)
THE SUN SALUTATION

CALORIES

Giver 62

Receiver 49

EQUIPMENT

Pillow

- ○ Below Average
- ○ Average
- ○ Above Average
- ○ Whoa!

COMMENTS

NOVEMBER 20)

THE "WHEEEE!"

CALORIES

Giver 117.6

Receiver 120

EQUIPMENT

Rocking Chair

- ○ Below Average
- ○ Average
- ○ Above Average
- ○ Whoa!

COMMENTS

____

____

____

____

____

____

NOVEMBER 21)
GET A LEG UP

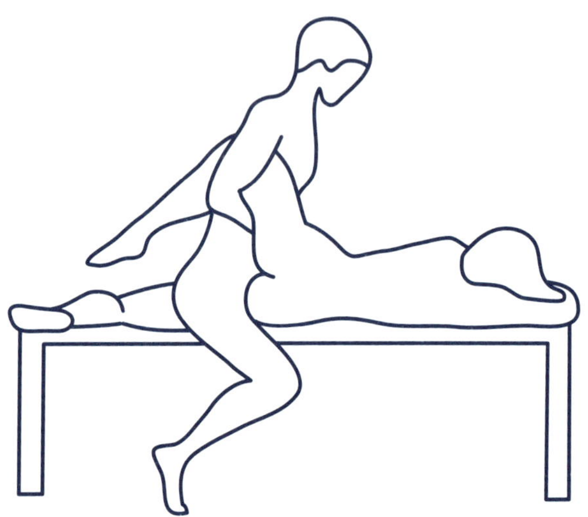

CALORIES
Giver 75.6
Receiver 48

EQUIPMENT
Bench

- ○ Below Average
- ○ Average
- ○ Above Average
- ○ Whoa!

COMMENTS

NOVEMBER 22)

THE ANGLER

CALORIES

Giver 100.8

Receiver 96

- ○ Below Average
- ○ Average
- ○ Above Average
- ○ Whoa!

COMMENTS

NOVEMBER 23)
THE SCRUNCHEE

CALORIES

Giver 75.6

Receiver 54

- ○ Below Average
- ○ Average
- ○ Above Average
- ○ Whoa!

COMMENTS

NOVEMBER 24)

THE HOVERCRAFT

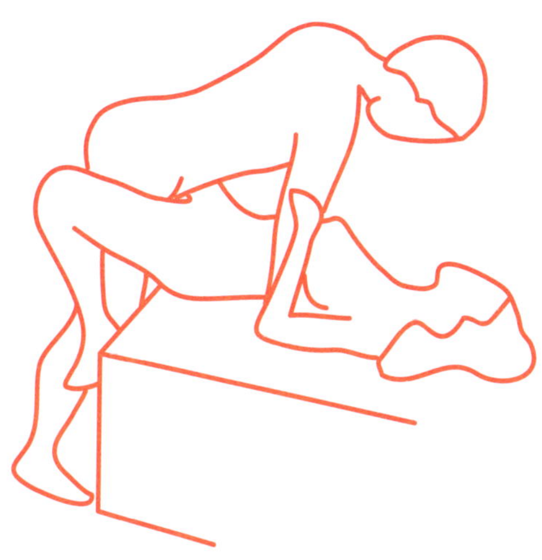

CALORIES

Giver 75.6

Receiver 54

EQUIPMENT

Bed

- ○ Below Average
- ○ Average
- ○ Above Average
- ○ Whoa!

COMMENTS

NOVEMBER 25)
THE ALL UP IN IT

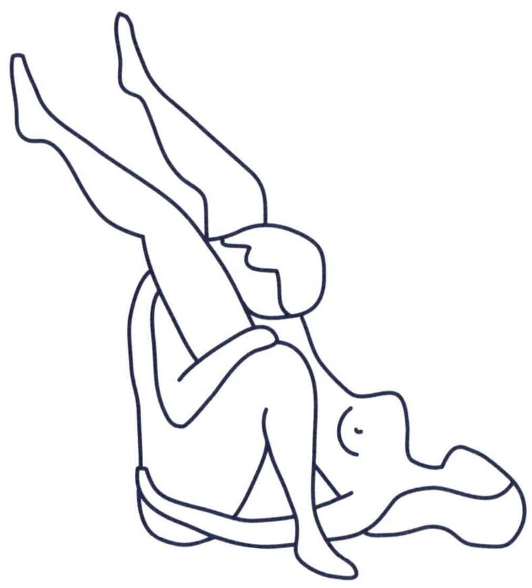

CALORIES

Giver 67.2

Receiver 96

- ○ Below Average
- ○ Average
- ○ Above Average
- ○ Whoa!

COMMENTS

NOVEMBER 26)

THE START OF A BEAUTIFUL FRIENDSHIP

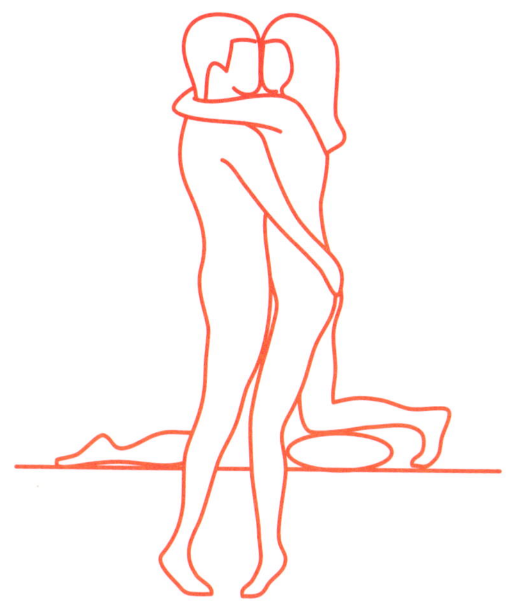

CALORIES

Giver 19.19

Receiver 13.6

EQUIPMENT

Bench

Pillow

○ Below Average

○ Average

○ Above Average

○ Whoa!

COMMENTS

____

____

____

____

____

____

NOVEMBER 27)

THE PERFORMANCE PIECE

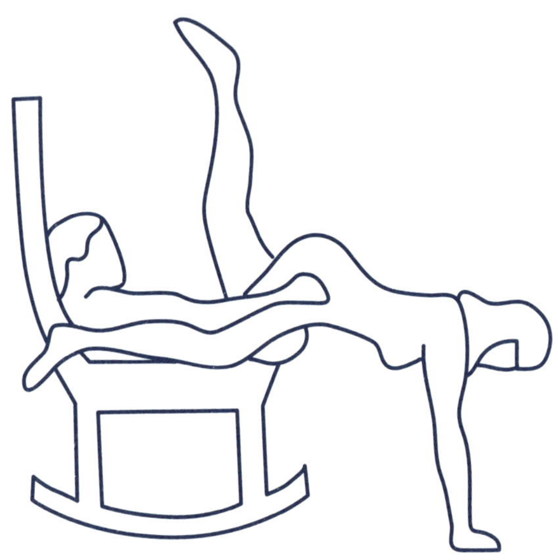

CALORIES

Giver 50

Receiver 78

EQUIPMENT

Rocking Chair

- ○ Below Average
- ○ Average
- ○ Above Average
- ○ Whoa!

COMMENTS

NOVEMBER 28)
THE COMPLEXITY OF DESIRE

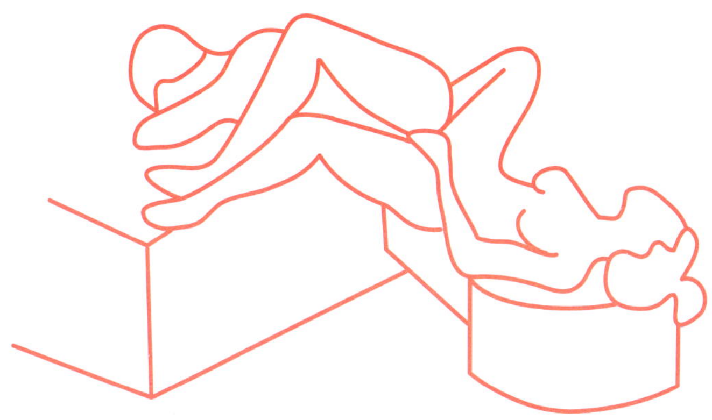

CALORIES		EQUIPMENT	
Giver	75.6	Stool	○ Below Average
Receiver	48	Bed	○ Average
			○ Above Average
			○ Whoa!

COMMENTS

NOVEMBER 29)
THE COBRA

CALORIES
Giver 72
Receiver 56

EQUIPMENT
Rocking Chair

- ○ Below Average
- ○ Average
- ○ Above Average
- ○ Whoa!

COMMENTS

NOVEMBER 30)
ON THE HORIZON

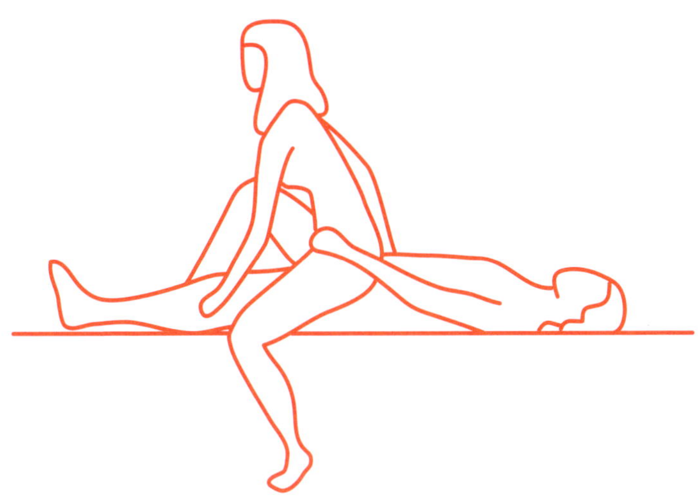

CALORIES

Giver	19
Receiver	48

- ○ Below Average
- ○ Average
- ○ Above Average
- ○ Whoa!

COMMENTS

DECEMBER 01)
THE X-MAS COUNTDOWN

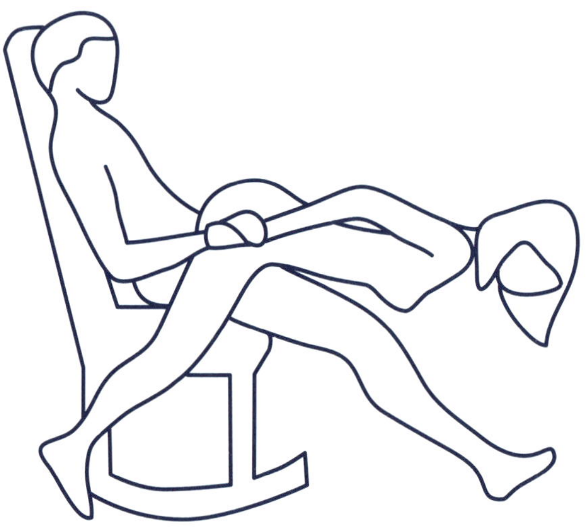

CALORIES

Giver 19

Receiver 48

EQUIPMENT

Rocking Chair

- ○ Below Average
- ○ Average
- ○ Above Average
- ○ Whoa!

COMMENTS

DECEMBER 02)

THE BUCKING BRONCO

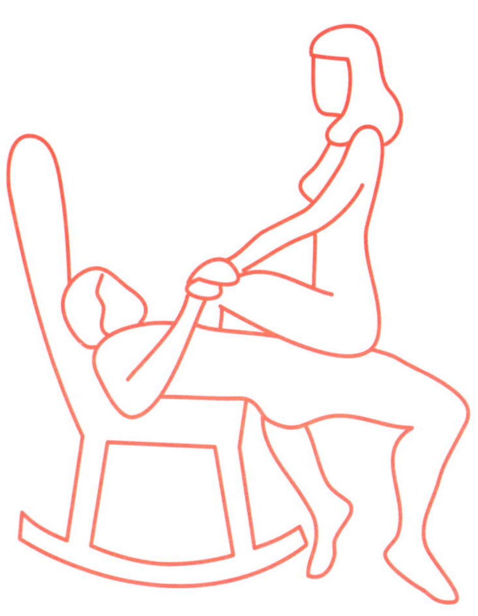

CALORIES		EQUIPMENT
Giver	19	Rocking Chair
Receiver	66	

- ○ Below Average
- ○ Average
- ○ Above Average
- ○ Whoa!

COMMENTS

____

____

____

____

____

____

DECEMBER 03)

THE OPEN-FACED SANDWICH

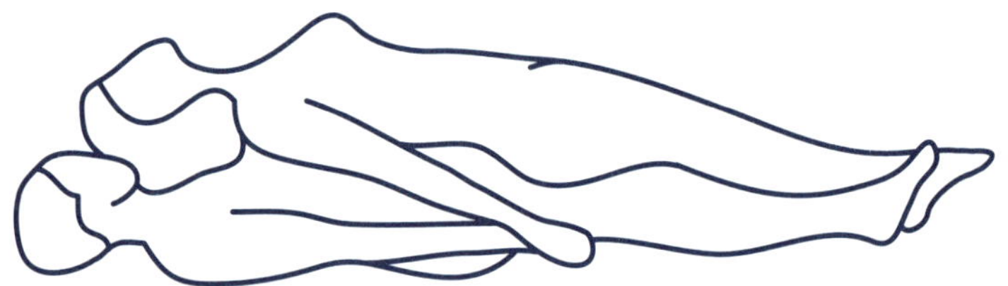

CALORIES

Giver 67.2

Receiver 48

- ○ Below Average
- ○ Average
- ○ Above Average
- ○ Whoa!

COMMENTS

DECEMBER 04)
THE FIRESIDE CHAT

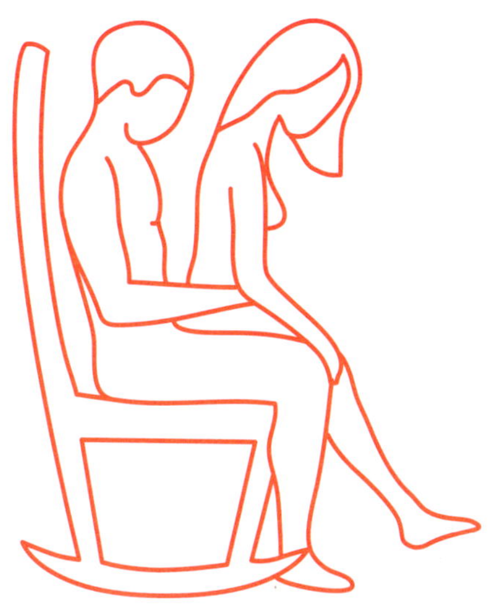

CALORIES
Giver 19
Receiver 54

EQUIPMENT
Rocking Chair
Optional:
Firewood

○ Below Average
○ Average
○ Above Average
○ Whoa!

COMMENTS

DECEMBER 05)
THE SNOWBALL EFFECT

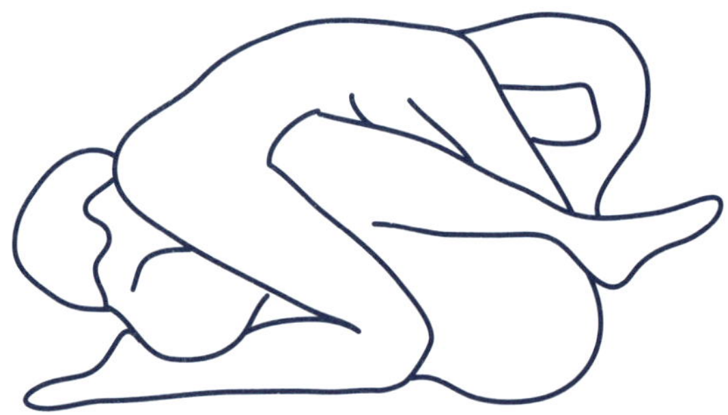

CALORIES

Giver 67.2

Receiver 48

- ○ Below Average
- ○ Average
- ○ Above Average
- ○ Whoa!

COMMENTS

____

____

____

____

____

____

DECEMBER 06)
THE HEADACHE CURE

CALORIES		EQUIPMENT	BENEFIT
Giver	75.6	Rocking Chair	Saves Money on Aspirin
Receiver	58	Stool	

- ○ Below Average
- ○ Average
- ○ Above Average
- ○ Whoa!

COMMENTS

____

____

____

____

____

____

DECEMBER 07)

THE “CATCH ME, I’M FALLING”

CALORIES

Giver 100.8

Receiver 96

EQUIPMENT

Bed

- ○ Below Average
- ○ Average
- ○ Above Average
- ○ Whoa!

COMMENTS

____

____

____

____

____

____

DECEMBER 08)

THE ANXIOUS HONEYMOONER

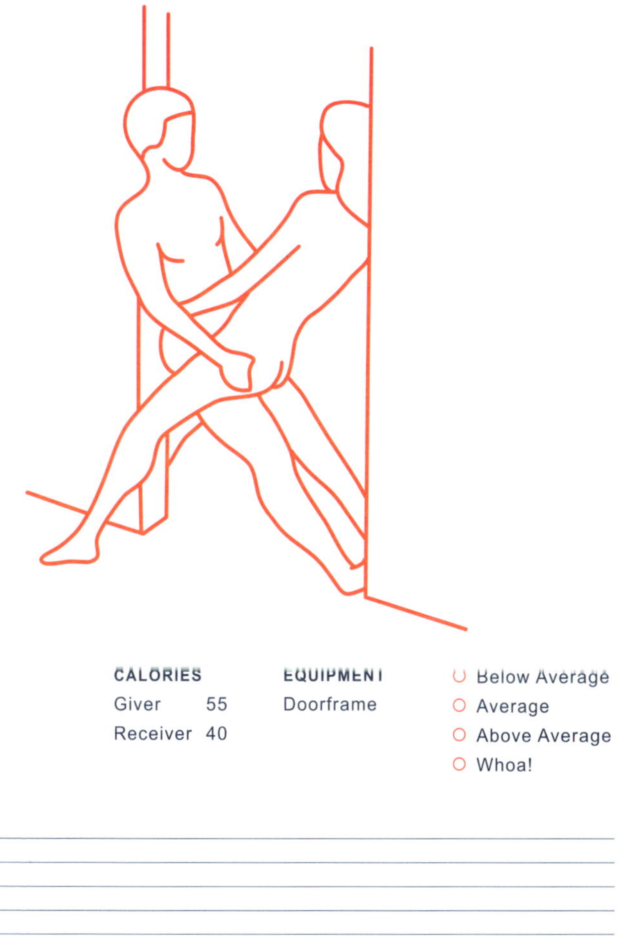

CALORIES

Giver 55

Receiver 40

EQUIPMENT

Doorframe

- ○ Below Average
- ○ Average
- ○ Above Average
- ○ Whoa!

COMMENTS

DECEMBER 09)
THE TAKE A LOAD OFF

CALORIES

Giver 84

Receiver 54

EQUIPMENT

Ottoman

- ○ Below Average
- ○ Average
- ○ Above Average
- ○ Whoa!

COMMENTS

DECEMBER 10)
BACK IT UP

CALORIES

Giver 19

Receiver 66

- ○ Below Average
- ○ Average
- ○ Above Average
- ○ Whoa!

COMMENTS

DECEMBER 11)

THE SPOON SWOON

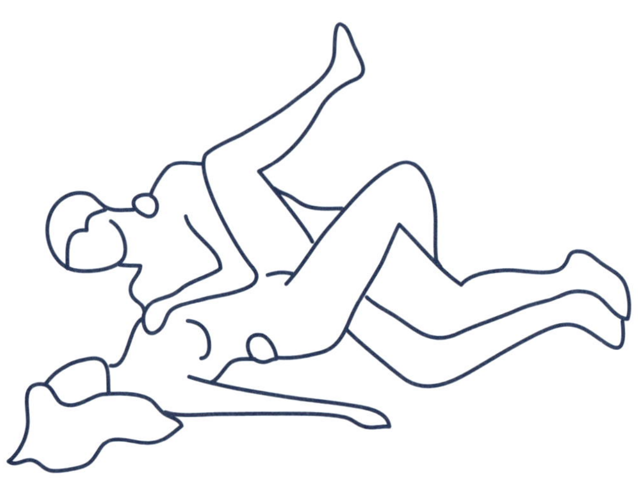

CALORIES

Giver 75.6

Receiver 54

○ Below Average

○ Average

○ Above Average

○ Whoa!

COMMENTS

DECEMBER 12)
THE GRAND CANYON

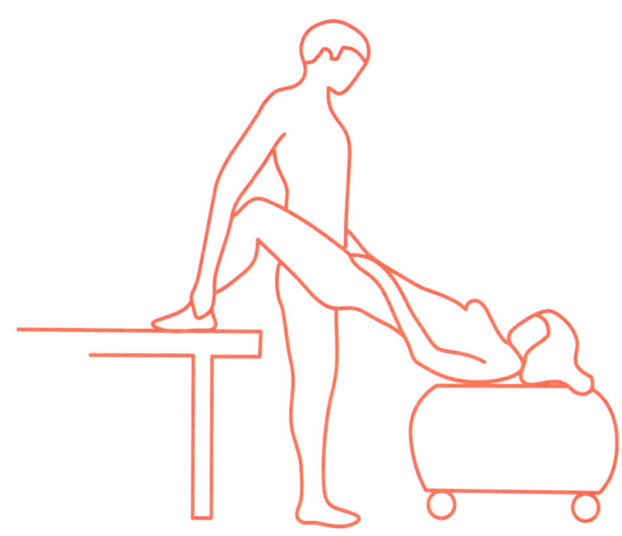

CALORIES		EQUIPMENT
Giver	75.6	Table
Receiver	96	Ottoman

○ Below Average
○ Average
○ Above Average
○ Whoa!

COMMENTS

DECEMBER 13)

THE THIGH HIGH

CALORIES

Giver 75.6

Receiver 54

○ Below Average

○ Average

○ Above Average

○ Whoa!

COMMENTS

DECEMBER 14)
REACHING FOR THE STARS

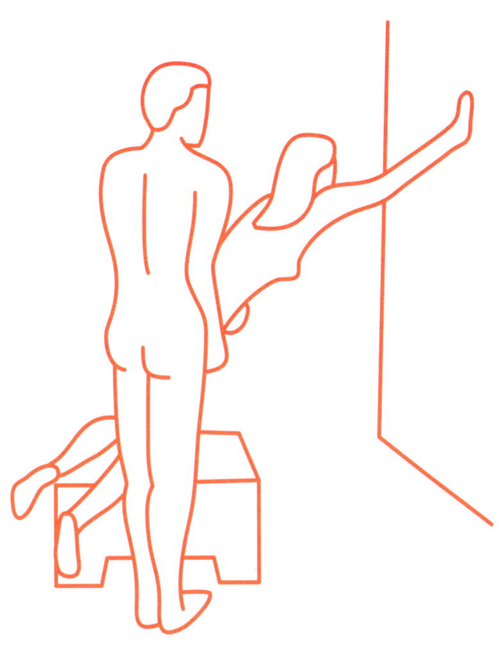

CALORIES		EQUIPMENT	
Giver	67.2	Stool	○ Below Average
Receiver	96	Wall	○ Average
			○ Above Average
			○ Whoa!

COMMENTS

DECEMBER 15)
ADVANCED TIC-TAC-TOE

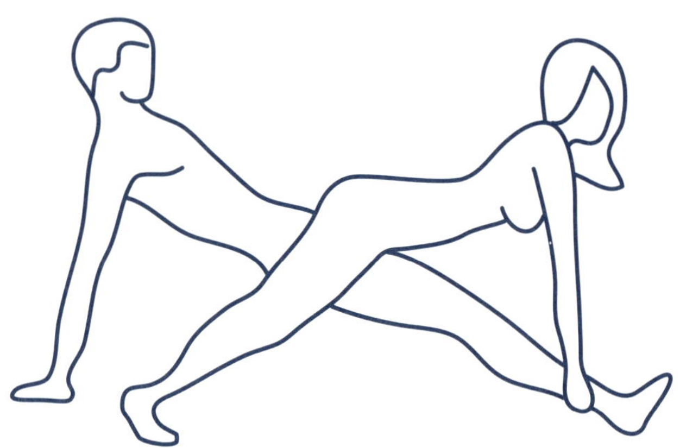

CALORIES

Giver 134.4

Receiver 96

- ○ Below Average
- ○ Average
- ○ Above Average
- ○ Whoa!

COMMENTS

DECEMBER 16)
YOU BLINKED

CALORIES

Giver 39

Receiver 28

- ○ Below Average
- ○ Average
- ○ Above Average
- ○ Whoa!

COMMENTS

DECEMBER 17)
RIBBED FOR YOUR PLEASURE

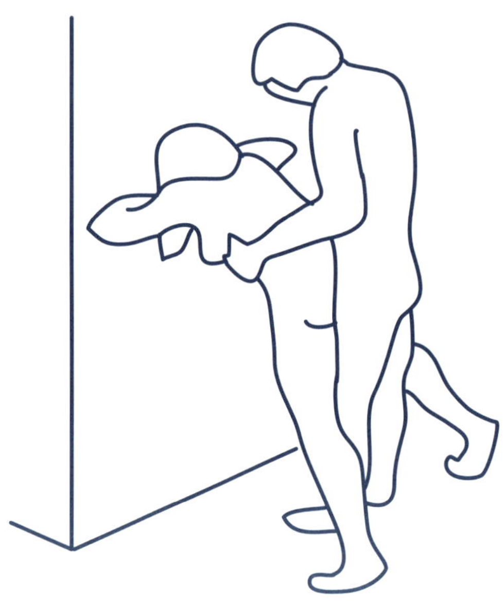

CALORIES

Giver 75.6

Receiver 54

EQUIPMENT

Wall

- ○ Below Average
- ○ Average
- ○ Above Average
- ○ Whoa!

COMMENTS

DECEMBER 18)
THE STARTING BLOCK

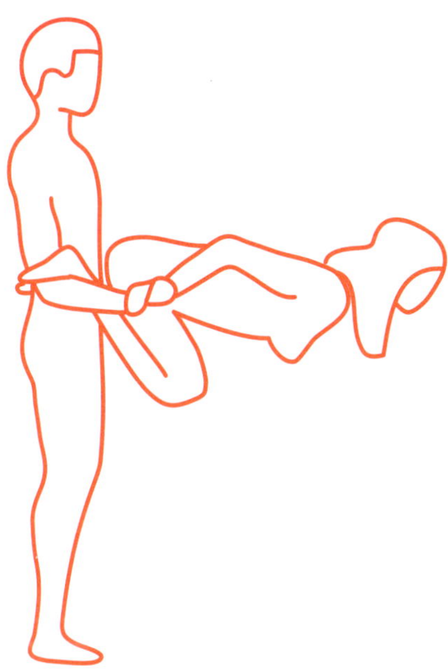

CALORIES	
Giver	100.8
Receiver	132

- ○ Below Average
- ○ Average
- ○ Above Average
- ○ Whoa!

COMMENTS

DECEMBER 19)

THE TEXAS HOLD 'EM

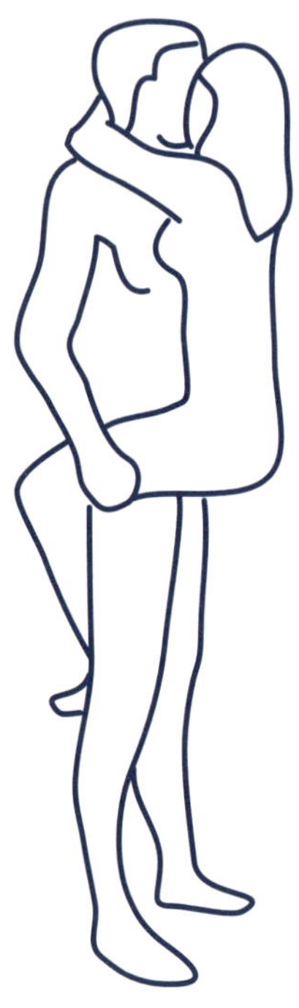

CALORIES

Giver 100.8

Receiver 66

- ○ Below Average
- ○ Average
- ○ Above Average
- ○ Whoa!

COMMENTS

DECEMBER 20)

THE ASKING YOUR EX TO LEAVE

CALORIES

Giver 134.4

Receiver 72

- ○ Below Average
- ○ Average
- ○ Above Average
- ○ Whoa!

COMMENTS

DECEMBER 21)
THE JOINT EFFORT

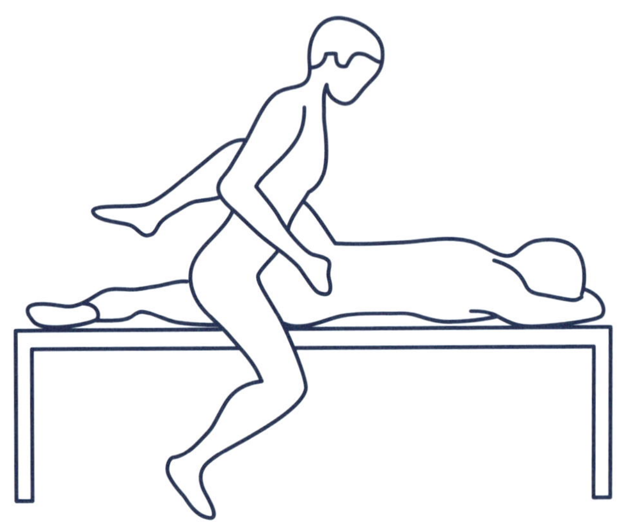

CALORIES		EQUIPMENT	BENEFIT	
Giver	75.6	Lotion	Loose Muscles	○ Below Average
Receiver	19	Massage Table		○ Average
				○ Above Average
				○ Whoa!

COMMENTS

DECEMBER 22)

THE SPECIAL DELIVERY

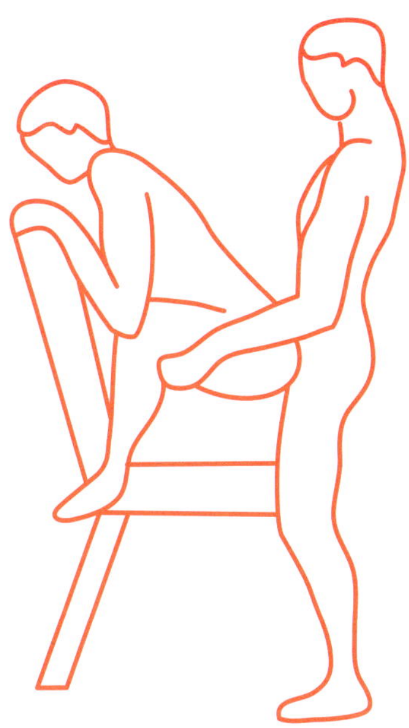

CALORIES

Giver 134

Receiver 75.6

- ○ Below Average
- ○ Average
- ○ Above Average
- ○ Whoa!

COMMENTS

DECEMBER 23)
THE PRE-GAME WARMUP

CALORIES		EQUIPMENT	BENEFIT	
Giver	67.2	Bench	Loose Hamstrings	○ Below Average
Receiver	66	Optional:		○ Average
		Pull-Off Basketball Jumpsuit		○ Above Average
				○ Whoa!

COMMENTS

DECEMBER 24)

THE NOSY NEIGHBOR

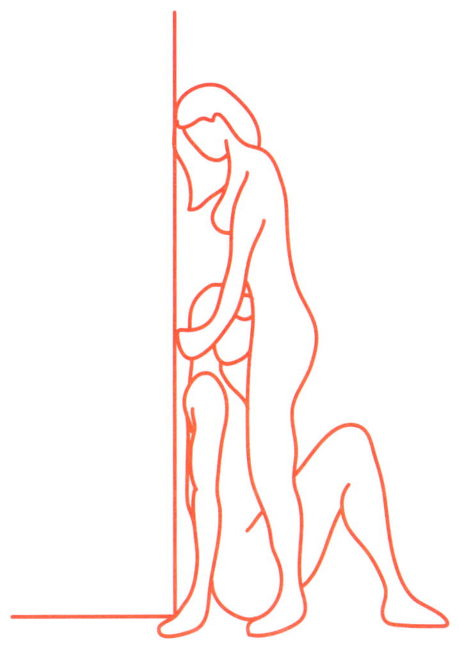

CALORIES

Giver 19

Receiver 48

EQUIPMENT

Wall

○ Below Average

○ Average

○ Above Average

○ Whoa!

COMMENTS

___

___

___

___

___

___

DECEMBER 25)
THE MERRY X-MAS

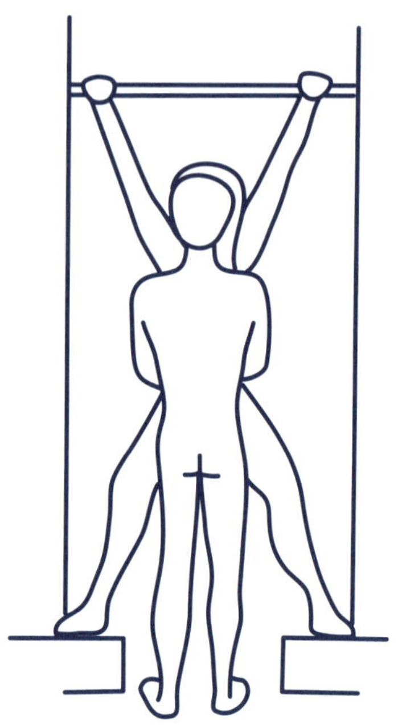

CALORIES		EQUIPMENT	BENEFIT	
Giver	75.6	Pull-Up Bar	No Christmas Shopping	○ Below Average
Receiver	48	Doorframe		○ Average
		Two Stools		○ Above Average
				○ Whoa!

COMMENTS

DECEMBER 26)

THE TRIPOD

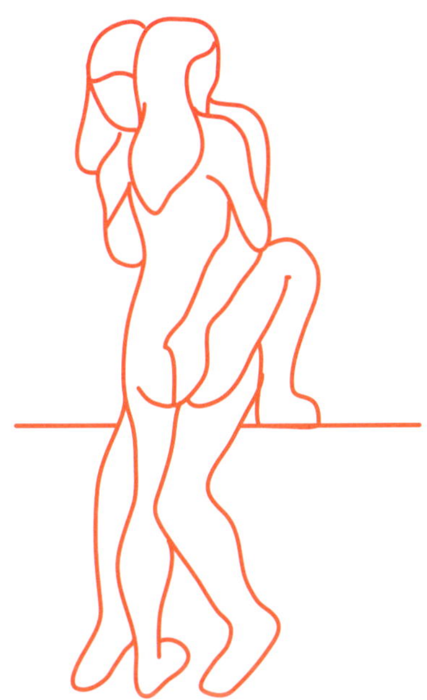

CALORIES

Giver/Receiver (One-Legged) 72

Giver/Receiver (Two-Legged) 55

EQUIPMENT

Bed

- ○ Below Average
- ○ Average
- ○ Above Average
- ○ Whoa!

COMMENTS

____

____

____

____

____

____

DECEMBER 27)
THE WELCOME HOME

CALORIES
Giver 66
Receiver 75.6

EQUIPMENT
Doorframe

○ Below Average
○ Average
○ Above Average
○ Whoa!

COMMENTS

DECEMBER 28)

THE BEAST WITH TWO BACKS

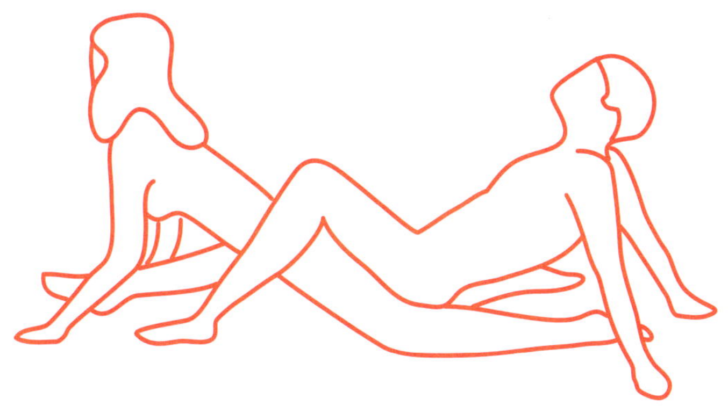

CALORIES

Giver 84

Receiver 61

- ○ Below Average
- ○ Average
- ○ Above Average
- ○ Whoa!

COMMENTS

____

____

____

____

____

____

DECEMBER 29)
THE ELEVATED DOGGY

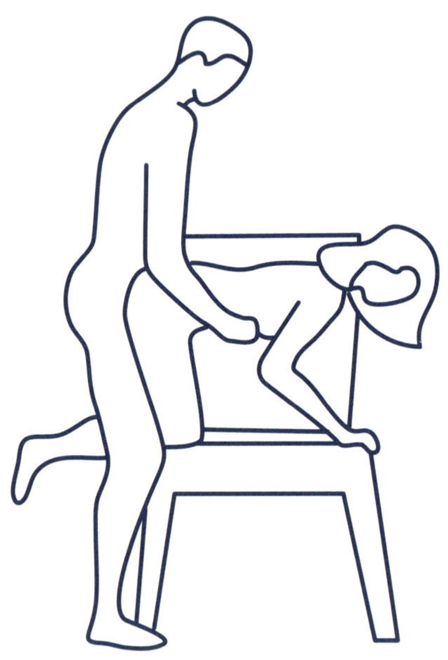

CALORIES

Giver 72

Receiver 56

EQUIPMENT

Chair

- ○ Below Average
- ○ Average
- ○ Above Average
- ○ Whoa!

COMMENTS

DECEMBER 30)
THE RAW BAR

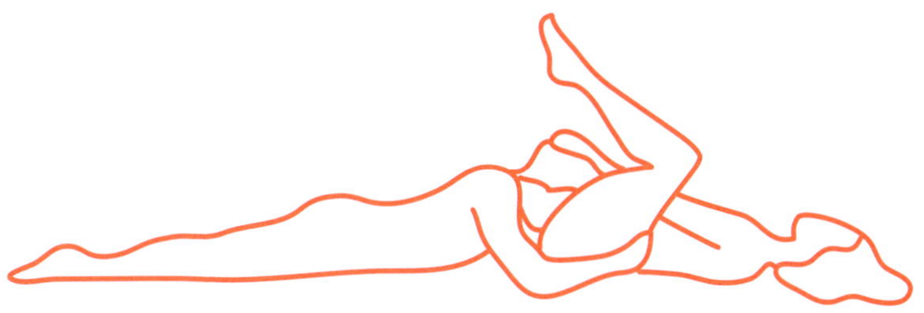

CALORIES

Giver	19
Receiver	48

- ○ Below Average
- ○ Average
- ○ Above Average
- ○ Whoa!

COMMENTS

DECEMBER 31)
SHOULD AULD ACQUAINTANCE BE FORGOT

CALORIES

Giver 19

Receiver 39

○ Below Average

○ Average

○ Above Average

○ Whoa!

COMMENTS

COMMENTS